These Truths

Catholicism and American Political Life

A Symposium With

David J. O'Brien, Ph.D., Kristin E. Heyer, Ph.D.,
Reverend Michael J. Himes, Ph.D.,
Reverend Kenneth R. Himes, O.F.M., Ph.D.,
Lisa Sowle Cahill, Ph.D.,
Reverend Drew Christiansen, S.J., Ph.D.

Edited by Richard W. Miller, Ph.D.

Liguori
Liguori, Missouri

Imprimi Potest:
Thomas D. Picton, C.Ss.R.
Provincial, Denver Province
The Redemptorists

ISBN 978-0-7648-1720-5

Liguori Publications, a nonprofit corporation, is an apostolate of the Redemptorists. To learn more about the Redemptorists, visit Redemptorists.com.

To order, call 800-325-9521
www.liguori.org

Printed in the United States of America
11 10 09 08 4 3 2 1

Contents

Introduction

Richard W. Miller, Ph.D., Assistant Professor of Systematic Theology, Creighton University

Every four years since 1976, the United States Conference of Catholic Bishops has published a document titled "Faithful Citizenship: A Catholic Call to Political Responsibility." "Faithful Citizenship" provides guidelines for Catholic engagement in public life. In accord with those guidelines, this year's conference draws on the expertise of distinguished American theologians to present background for Catholic engagement in American public life.

The central purpose of the conference is to explore the fundamental principles of Catholic doctrine in light of contemporary political, moral, and social life in the United States. The first three papers are primarily concerned with moral principles and historical background. The next three papers focus on the application of these principles to concrete political and social issues. The first paper, *Catholicism and American Political Life: A Response to the Current Tendency to Narrow Catholic Social Teaching,* which is my own contribution, counters the tendency in the last presidential election to narrow Catholic social teaching. The second paper, *Fundamental Principles: Conscience, Religion, and Politics,* by Michael Himes, clarifies several fundamental principles at the heart of the relationship between Catholicism and American political life by exploring the meaning of the words *religion, politics,* and *conscience.* The third paper, *History of Catholicism in American Politics,* by David O'Brien, contextualizes the contemporary situation and the emergence of the document "Faithful Citizenship" within the larger history of U.S. Catholicism. The fourth paper, *The Common Good and the American Bishops' Guidelines,* by Kristin Heyer, examines the notion of the common good and indicates how the common good should shape political discernment on the issues of economic justice and immigration. The fifth paper, *Working for Peace,* by Kenneth Himes, O.F.M., explores the meaning of peace, the contemporary developments within Catholic social teaching on peace, the recent emergence of the notion of peacebuilding, and questions that must be considered by U.S. Catholics concerning the ethics of war and peace. The sixth paper, *Protection of Life,* by Lisa Cahill, counters the tendency among Catholics to view life issues in terms of individual rights, decisions, and responsibilities by arguing that the protection of life requires a strong social ethics and ethics of the common good. The seventh paper, *Catholic Environmentalism*, by Drew Christiansen, S.J., explores the application of the principle of the common good to environmental issues. The hope is that these papers and the lively panel discussion that follows them will provide people with some sense of the resources that the Catholic tradition holds for addressing pressing public questions.

1. A Response to the Tendency to Narrow Catholic Social Teaching

Richard W. Miller, Ph.D., Creighton University

In recent years, the influence in American public life of the religious beliefs and values of Christians has been quite pronounced. Those who designate themselves "evangelical Protestants" have become a highly influential voting block in American politics. They represent 24 percent of the population and according to the Pew Forum on Religion and Public Life, "White evangelical Christians…form a distinct group whose members share core religious beliefs as well as crystallized and consistently conservative political attitudes."[1] Their political cohesiveness was witnessed in the last presidential election. In 2004, 78 percent of white evangelical Protestants voted for President Bush[2] and they represented 40 percent of President Bush's votes.[3]

How do evangelical Protestants understand the relation of their Christian faith to American public life and American democracy? Sixty-two percent of white evangelical Protestants think everything in the Bible is literally true,[4] and 60 percent of them maintain that "the Bible should be the guiding principle in making laws when it conflicts with the will of the people."[5] These are very significant numbers. The percentage of white evangelical Protestants who think the Bible should be the guiding principle in making laws is significantly higher than the percentage of Muslims in Pakistan or Egypt or Morocco who think that Sharia law should be strictly applied in Muslim countries.[6] Sharia law,

1. The Pew Research Center for the People and the Press and the Pew Forum on Religion and Public Life, "Many Americans Uneasy With the Mix of Religion and Politics: 69% Say Liberals Are Too Secular, 49% Say Conservatives Are Too Assertive" (Aug. 24, 2006), 3, http://pewforum.org/publications/surveys/religion-politics-06.pdf.
2. The Pew Research Center for the People and the Press and the Pew Forum on Religion and Public Life, "The American Religious Landscape and the 2004 Presidential Vote: Increased Polarization" (Nov.-Dec., 2004), 2, http://pewforum.org/publications/surveys/postelection.pdf.
3. Ibid., 2.
4. Pew Research Center and Pew Forum, "Many Americans Uneasy With Mix of Religion and Politics," 19.
5. Ibid., 2.
6. Steven Kull, Clay Ramsay, Stephen Weber, Evan Lewis, Ebrahim Mohseni, Mary Speck, Melanie Ciolek, Melinda Brouwer, "Muslim Public Opinion on US Policy, Attacks on Civilians and al Qaeda" (College Park, MD: The Program on International Policy Attitudes, April 24, 2007), 21, http://www.worldpublicopinion.org/pipa/pdf/apr07/START_Apr07_rpt.pdf.

as you recall, refers in Islam to God's divine law as revealed in the Koran and through the example and teachings of the prophet Muhammed.

If evangelical Protestants exercise such an enormous political influence, where do Catholics stand in relation to American political life? The answer to this question will be developed throughout the day, but let me start with a sampling of social scientific data. In the last presidential election, 52 percent of Catholics voted for George Bush and 47 percent voted for John Kerry.[7] More than 80 percent of Catholics think the Bible is the Word of God, but only about a quarter of all Catholics think the Bible should be read literally and should be the guiding principle in making laws when it conflicts with the will of the people.[8]

What explains the difference between evangelical Protestants and Catholics? There are a number of factors, but one central and classical difference is the question of the interpretation of Scripture, and by extension, the understanding of "church." Going back to Martin Luther, the tendency in Protestantism is to privilege Scripture as interpreted through the individual believer. In Catholicism, the tendency is to read Scripture through official Church teaching. If asked about the view of their faith on a particular issue, Protestants tend to quote Scripture and maybe the authority of their minister. Catholics, however, tend to think in terms of Church teaching. Here "Church" is often understood not in its proper sense as the people of God, but more in terms of one aspect of the Church, namely, the teaching office of the community.

If Catholics look to the teaching of the magisterium as defining the beliefs of the Catholic faith, how do contemporary Catholics understand magisterial teaching in relation to political life? From the 2004 presidential election, one cannot help but suspect that for the majority of the nearly seventy-seven million Catholics in the United States, the dominant impression is that official Church teaching is concerned only with one issue or a handful of issues. This perception was fueled by the media's attention to the statements of a few bishops. In 2004 several bishops maintained publicly that John Kerry and other Catholic politicians should not be allowed to receive Communion because they

7. Cable News Network, "Election Results," http:/www.cnn.com/ELECTION/2004/pages/results/states/US/P/00/epolls.0.html (accessed May 28, 2007).

8. Pew Research Center and Pew Forum, "Many Americans Uneasy With Mix of Religion and Politics," 2.

were running on a pro-choice platform. Some bishops also suggested that it would be a sin for a Catholic to vote for a politician running on a pro-choice platform.[9] In his retrospective reporting on the issue, Peter Steinfels, the religion editor of *The New York Times,* put it this way, "In the end, a handful of outspoken bishops, their stance predictably magnified in news reports, successfully established the hierarchy's election-year profile."[10] These outspoken bishops and the perception generated by their comments represented neither the majority opinion of the bishops in the United States nor the explicit teaching of the United States Conference of Catholics Bishops (USCCB).[11]

"Faithful Citizenship" was published in 2003. Citing the Congregation for the Doctrine of the Faith, the document states:

> *The Christian faith is an integral unity, and thus it is incoherent to isolate some particular element to the detriment of the whole of Catholic doctrine. A political commitment to a single isolated aspect of the Church's social doctrine does not exhaust one's responsibility towards the common good.*[12]

> *[The Church] does not wish to exercise political power or eliminate the freedom of opinion of Catholics regarding contingent questions. Instead, it intends—as is its proper function—to instruct and illuminate the consciences of the faithful, particularly those involved in political life, so that their actions may always serve the integral promotion of the human person and the common good.*[13]

---

9. Patricia Zapor, "Postelection reflection: Bishops talk about Communion and politicians," *Catholic News Service,* Nov. 18, 2004.

10. Peter Steinfels, "Beliefs; Persuasion or penalties? In delicate tug-of-faith with Catholic politicians, velvet glove is in for now," *The New York Times,* June 24, 2006.

11. Ibid.

12. U.S. Conference of Catholic Bishops, "Faithful Citizenship: A Catholic Call to Political Responsibility" (Washington, DC: USCCB, 2003), 12 [EDITOR'S NOTE: References to "Faithful Citizenship" herein are from the 2003 document (the 2007 version of the document is available at http://www.usccb.org/faithfulcitizenship)]. "Faithful Citizenship" is citing The Congregation for the Doctrine of the Faith, "Doctrinal Note on some questions regarding the participation of Catholics in political life" (November, 24, 2002), no. 4, http://www.vatican.va/roman_curia/congregations/cfaith/documents/rc_con_cfaith_doc_20021124_politica_en.html.

13. "Faithful Citizenship," 11. "Faithful Citizenship" is citing The Congregation for the Doctrine of the Faith, "Doctrinal Note on some questions regarding the participation of Catholics in political life," no. 6.

In an effort to instruct and inform the development of the consciences of the people of God, "Faithful Citizenship" highlights more than fifty different issues that must be considered when Catholics engage in public life. We certainly will not be able to deal with all these issues today. We should, however, at least hear the range of issues that we are being asked to consider in order to counteract the tendency to narrow Catholic social teaching. The bishops develop these fifty different issues under four general moral priorities.[14]

The first moral priority is protecting human life. Under this moral priority the bishops ask us to consider the following issues: abortion, assisted suicide and euthanasia, cloning, intentional targeting of civilians in war or terrorist attacks, biotechnology, avoiding war, preemptive or preventive use of force, nuclear weapons, antipersonnel land mines, global trade in arms, and the death penalty.

The second moral priority is promoting family life. Under this moral priority, the bishops ask us to consider the following: marriage, just wages, the protection of children, the education of children, the right to choose in education, the media and the common good, the problem of media concentration, and the problem of offensive television and Internet content.

The third moral priority is pursuing social justice. Under this moral priority, the bishops ask us to consider the following: economic justice; jobs for all who can work; a living wage; unjust discrimination; the right of workers to choose to organize; economic freedom, initiative, and the right to private property; welfare reform as a way to reduce poverty; child tax credits to help bring people out of poverty; support of the work of faith-based groups; the reform of Social Security; affordable and accessible health care as a fundamental human right; reform of the nation's health care system; safe and affordable housing; agriculture policies that provide food security for all; a living wage for farmers and farm workers; sustainable agriculture, stewardship of the earth and its natural resources; solidarity with immigrants both documented and undocumented "[w]hile affirming the right and responsibility of sovereign nations to control their borders and to ensure the security of their citizens"[15]; the right to a quality education; just wages for teachers and

14. The following list of issues are treated in "Faithful Citizenship," 9–15.
15. "Faithful Citizenship," 24.

administrators; the funding of services for at-risk students in public, private, or religious schools; the culture of violence in the media; gun safety measures and restrictions; the death penalty; reform of the criminal justice system; the support of "judiciously administered affirmative action"; care for the environment; and global climate change.

The fourth moral priority is practicing global solidarity. The following concerns fall under this moral priority: understanding national security only in terms of militarism, poverty and underdevelopment, and the humanizing of globalization; global poverty; promotion of religious liberty and other basic human rights; the spread of nuclear, chemical, and biological weapons; consistent support for appropriate United Nations programs and other international bodies; support for international law; offering asylum to those fleeing persecution; adoption of a more generous immigration and refugee policy; collaboration with the international community in addressing regional conflicts; providing leadership on the Israeli-Palestinian conflict; and sustained commitment to Iraq and Afghanistan.[16]

The reading of this list is not exactly lyrical, but it is important that we lay all these issues on the table so that we at least recognize the panorama we are asked to consider as responsible Catholics. I think that many resist taking seriously the bishops' insistence that there are more than fifty issues to consider because they are afraid that if we take these other issues seriously, we will be diverting attention from the scourge that is abortion. Indeed, in the 2004 presidential election and the 2006 congressional elections the 2003 bishops' document "Faithful Citizenship" received some stiff competition. A San Diego–based group called Catholic Answers Actions distributed ten million pamphlets, titled "Voter's Guide for Serious Catholics," to parishes across the country.

16. In order to avoid confusion, it should be noted that the notion of "a sustained commitment to Iraq and Afghanistan" has been further nuanced by the bishops on Jan. 12, 2007. In that report the bishops reiterate their own statements and John Paul II's statements expressing the grave moral concerns they had prior to the war. They indicate that our future actions in Iraq should be evaluated in terms of "our nation's moral responsibility to help Iraqis to live with security and dignity in the aftermath of U.S. military action. Our nation's military forces should remain in Iraq only as long as their presence actually contributes to a responsible transition. Our nation should seek effective ways to end their deployment at the earliest opportunity consistent with this goal." Bishop William S. Skylstad, "Evaluating Plans for a Responsible Transition in Iraq: A Statement of the President of the United States Conference of Catholic Bishops" (Washington, DC: USCCB, January 12, 2007), http://www.usccb.org/sdwp/international/20070112iraqstm.pdf.

These pamphlets argued that Catholic voters should cast their votes not in terms of reflection on the fifty-plus issues outlined in the bishops' document "Faithful Citizenship," but in terms of a candidate's position on five nonnegotiable issues: abortion, euthanasia, embryonic stem cell research, human cloning, and same-sex marriage."[17] Abortion heads this highly restricted list and looms largely throughout the pamphlet.[18] In addition, the pro-life agenda of the pamphlet is further narrowed to the tactic of making abortion illegal.

Abortion always casts a long shadow over these discussions and seems to eclipse the myriad of issues that we are asked to consider in "Faithful Citizenship." This conference would like to give attendees a sense of the panorama of issues that the bishops ask to consider as a part of Catholic social teaching and then focus in depth on a handful of issues. It is not a conference on abortion. Abortion alone, as with each of these fifty issues, could occupy a daylong conference. While this is not a conference on abortion, I want to clarify in the opening talk that in dealing with an array of other issues, we are not sidestepping, downplaying, or even ignoring the scourge that is abortion.

In "Faithful Citizenship," the bishops devote a paragraph to abortion in the section dealing with the fifty issues that we are to consider. After maintaining that "[a]bortion, the deliberate killing of a human being before birth, is never morally acceptable,"[19] the bishops devote two sentences to recommendations for responding to the problem of abortion. In the first sentence they recognize that we should approach the tragedy of abortion by trying to make it illegal: "We support constitutional protection for unborn human life, as well as legislative efforts to end abortion and euthanasia."[20] In the second they suggest that we work to eliminate abortions by offering a safety net for preg-

17. Peter Steinfels, "Voters' Guides Define Moral Compromises to Take to Polls," *The New York Times*, October 14, 2006.

18. The pamphlet has two parts. First, it outlines principles and explains the five nonnegotiable issues. Second, it provides "practical advice about how to decide to cast your vote" (p. 4). In the practical advice section, there are three times when the pamphlet deals with the application of principles to particular issues. Two of the three times moral principles are brought to bear on particular issues, it deals only with abortion. The third time it applies principles to abortion together with euthanasia. Catholic Answers Action, "Voter's Guide for Serious Catholics" (El Cajon, CA: Catholic Answers Action, 2006), http://www.caaction.com/pdf/Voters-Guide-Catholic-English-1p.pdf.

19. "Faithful Citizenship," 17.

20. Ibid., 18.

nant mothers and education promoting childbirth and adoption: "We encourage the passage of laws and programs that promote childbirth and adoption over abortion and assist pregnant women and children."[21] Offering a safety net for pregnant mothers is connected to a number of other issues that the bishops ask us to consider: economic justice; jobs for all who can work; a living wage; welfare reform as a way to reduce poverty; child tax credits to help bring people out of poverty; affordable and accessible health care as a fundamental human right; reform of the nation's health care system; and safe and affordable housing.[22]

The bishops' second recommendation is supported by social scientific evidence. The places in the world with the lowest abortion rates are in Western Europe—Belgium, Germany, and the Netherlands.[23] This is a complex issue, but one important factor is that these countries have a social safety net so that a woman who has an unintended pregnancy is less likely to abort the fetus for economic reasons. The significance of welfare is also clear from U.S. data. Women living below the federal poverty level of $9,570 a year for a single woman with no children are four times more likely to have an abortion than women living at 300 percent of the poverty level, which is roughly $30,000 a year for a single woman with no children.[24] Welfare programs directly impact this issue

---

21. Ibid., 18.
22. Ibid., 12–13.
23. Susan A. Cohen, "Toward Making Abortion 'Rare': The Shifting Battleground over the Means to an End," *Guttmacher Policy Review*, vol. 9, no. 1 (Winter 2006), http://www.guttmacher.org/pubs/gpr/09/1/gpr090102.html.
24. Guttmacher Institute, "Facts on Induced Abortion in the United States," May 2006, http://www.guttmacher.org/pubs/fb_induced_abortion.html. The Guttmacher Institute was founded in 1968 to provide nonpartisan social scientifically based evidence to aid the government in forming policies and the public in assessing the sensitive issues of reproductive health and reproductive rights. Although the Guttmacher Institute was originally constituted as a semiautonomous division of Planned Parenthood, its data are considered the most accurate data on abortion numbers. Its data are accepted by pro-life organizations. For instance, the data are used by the National Right to Life (http://www.nrlc.org/abortion/aboramt.html) and the Center for Bioethical Reform (http://www.abortionno.org/Resources/fastfacts.html). According to the Guttmacher Institute, "Articles in the Institute's domestic and international journals undergo blinded peer review. The Guttmacher Institute neither accepts direct project support from profit-making organizations that might benefit from its findings nor allows specific funding agencies to influence its agenda." (http://www.guttmacher.org/about/faq.html). If one objects that these statistics must be biased because they come from the research arm of Planned Parenthood, then the only proper response is to establish a similar institute under pro-life auspices with data subjected to blinded peer review. The Guttmacher Institute has a staff of 61, many of them eminent professionals in their field, and an operating budget of $11 million a year.

because 95 percent of welfare recipients in the United States are women and children. In fact, "Federal welfare assistance was originally created in the 1930s to enable single mothers to care for their children at home, instead of losing them to foster homes or orphanages."[25] Federal spending on the welfare program, however, is less than 1 percent of the total federal budget.[26] Let me bring this issue of poverty closer to home. In the state of Missouri, 14 percent of families and 17 percent of children live in poverty. Across the street in Kansas, with its better schools and freedom from the ills that plague us on this side of state line, 14 percent of families and 16 percent of children live in poverty. They are basically the same; nearly 1 of every 6 children lives in poverty in Missouri and Kansas.

The bishops not only "encourage the passage of laws and programs that...assist pregnant women and children" but also "laws and programs that promote childbirth and adoption."[27] The current federal programs, however, are terribly underfunded. The Family Planning and Population Research Act of 1970 created the Family Planning program. This program has a dual role: to prevent unintended pregnancies through proper education and to counsel those who face an unintended pregnancy. While this program does counsel women on the use of contraception, which is counter to an element of Catholic teaching, it does not fund any programs where abortion is used as a method of family planning. When a woman is faced with an unintended pregnancy, she is informed of three options: prenatal care and delivery, foster care or adoption, and abortion. While abortion is an option by law, according to an article in the *Adoption Factbook*, published by the National Council For Adoption, this counseling setting increases the probability of a mother placing her child for adoption rather than choosing an abortion. Without this counseling the mother in all likelihood will not understand the adoption process and thus will not recognize adoption as a viable option. This program is inadequately financed such that an estimated 39% of women in need

25. National Priorities Project, "National Priorities Quick Report: Poverty in Missouri" http://nationalpriorities.org (accessed May 27, 2007).
26. Ibid.
27. "Faithful Citizenship," 18.

of this counseling are not being served.[28] Much needs to be done to make adoption a real option for women. Each year very few babies are placed for adoption relative to the number of abortions. In 2003, there were 848,163 legal induced abortions,[29] while only 14,000 children were placed for adoption.[30]

In considering the range of issues proposed by the bishops, abortion is taken quite seriously, for abortion is directly and indirectly related to many other issues. Directly it is related to social welfare issues. Indirectly it is related to all the other national issues because it bears upon our national priorities in terms of the federal budget. While social welfare programs make up 1 percent of the federal budget and family planning services that could reduce the number of abortions are underfunded, the United States spends 36 cents of every tax dollar in military spending.[31] Many experts suggest that we could cut billions of dollars in military spending without losing any security—for homeland security and preventive measures receive paltry funding relative to the military portion of our national security budget. Military spending makes up 89 percent of our national security budget, while homeland security and preventive measures only represent 11 percent of that budget.[32]

I have insisted, following the "Faithful Citizenship" document, that a pro-life position on abortion cannot be reduced simply to overturn-

---

28. Frank Bonati, "Pro-Choice Family Planning and Adoption: A Case to Strengthen Mutual Support" in *Adoption Factbook III*, eds. Connaught Marshner, William L. Pierce (Waite Park, MN: National Council for Adoption, 1999), 287–288, http://www.ncfa-usa.org/documents/AdoptionFactbook.pdf.

29. Lilo T. Strauss, Sonya B. Gamble, Wilda Y. Parker, Douglas A. Cook, Suzanne B. Zane, Saeed Hamdan, "Abortion Surveillance—United States 2003" (Atlanta, GA: Department of Health and Human Services Centers for Disease Control and Prevention, November 24, 2006/55(SS11), 1–32, http://www.cdc.gov/mmwr/preview/mmwrhtml/ss5511a1.htm. This number does not give a complete picture of the number of abortions in the United States because after 1997 California, and a few other states with smaller populations, have no longer reported the abortions in their respective states. This is why I use the 1997 data when possible.

30. Susan A. Cohen, "Toward Making Abortion 'Rare.'"

31. This includes present military spending of $0.28 and payment on the debt for military spending of $0.09 for every tax dollar spent. See National Priorities Project, "Where Do Your Tax Dollars Go?" http://www.nationalpriorities.org/index.php?option=com_content&task=view&id=286&Itemid=28 (accessed May 29, 2007).

32. See National Priorities Project, "National Security," http://www.nationalpriorities.org/index.php?option=com_content&task=view&id=97&Itemid=4 (accessed May 29, 2007).

ing *Roe v. Wade;* rather, it involves a whole host of other issues. I have corroborated with social scientific data the bishops' support of "the passage of laws and programs that promote childbirth and adoption over abortion and assist pregnant women and children."[33] In examining the social scientific data, another factor in limiting abortions leaps off the page. I hesitate to draw your attention to these data, but I would leave you with a false sense of the data if I did not include the information here. When I began my research, I did not expect to find that the central determining factor for the rate of abortions is not whether abortion is legal or illegal.

The lowest abortions rates in the world, as of the end of 2006, are in countries in Western Europe (Belgium, Germany, and the Netherlands) where abortion is legal, widely available, and is generally paid for by the national health care systems. On the other hand, some of the highest abortion rates in the world are in countries in South America where abortion is illegal.[34] These countries include Peru, Chile, and Brazil. In the extensive 1999 worldwide study, the Netherlands had the lowest abortion rate.[35] The abortion rate in Peru was nearly 7.5 times the Netherlands; Chile had an abortion rate that was nearly 6.5 times that of the Netherlands; and Brazil's abortion rate was 5 times the Netherlands with a maternal death rate 26 times that of the Netherlands. These figures are shocking data for Catholics—Peru, Chile, and Brazil are almost entirely Catholic. In fact, Brazil has the largest Catholic population in the world.

The data from worldwide studies suggest that the rate of abortions is not determined by whether abortion is legal. This fact also seems to be supported by data from the United States. The rate of abortions in 1967 before the federal legalization of abortion seems to have been

---

33. "Faithful Citizenship," 18.

34. These data are based on the extensive worldwide study done by the Guttmacher Institute in 1999: Guttmacher Institute, "Sharing Responsibility: Women, Society, and Abortion Worldwide" (New York: Guttmacher Institute, 1999). I have used the shorter summary of this study: Cynthia Dailard, "Abortion in Context: United States and Worldwide" (Guttmacher Institute, May 1999), http://www.guttmacher.org/pubs/ib_0599.html.

35. Since 1975, the Netherlands has consistently had the lowest or one of the lowest abortion rates in the world. See Stanley K. Henshaw, Susheela Singh, and Taylor Haas, "Recent Trends in Abortion Rates Worldwide," *International Family Planning Perspectives*, vol. 25, no. 1 (March 1999), table 1, http://www.guttmacher.org/pubs/journals/2504499.html.

slightly higher than the rate of abortions in 1997.[36] In 1967, an estimated 829,000 illegal abortions were performed in the United States[37] with an abortion rate of 21 abortions for every 1,000 women ages 15 through 44. In 1997, there were 1,186,039 abortions in the United States, with an abortion rate of 20 abortions for every 1,000 women ages 1 through 44.[38] Although there were more abortions in 1997 than 1967, the abortion rate in 1997 seems to have been slightly lower than in 1967 because there were nearly 20 million more women ages 15 through 44 in 1997 compared to 1967.[39]

If world and U.S. data suggest that the central factor determining the rate of abortions is not whether abortions are legal, then what is the central factor? According to Guttmacher Institute research, while "the reasons women have abortions transcend national boundaries, religions and cultures…the proximate cause is unplanned pregnancy, a common occurrence in the United States and abroad."[40] Worldwide there are an estimated 46 million unintended pregnancies. Forty percent of these

---

36. I have used the 1997 data because after 1997 the data were no longer reported from every state in the country. California is among the several states that have not reported since 1997. As the most populated state in the United States, California would change the numbers quite significantly. Laurie D. Elam-Evans, Lilo T. Strauss, Joy Herndon, Wilda Y. Parker, Sonya V. Bowens, Suzanne Zane, and Cynthia J. Berg, "Abortion Surveillance—United States 2000" (Atlanta, GA: Department of Health and Human Services Centers for Disease Control and Prevention, Nov. 28, 2003/52SS12; 1–2) table 2, http://www.cdc.gov/mmwr/preview/mmwrhtml/ss5212a1.htm.

37. According to an article in the Guttmacher Report in Public Policy, "Estimates of the number of illegal abortions in the 1950s and 1960s ranged from 200,000 to 1.2 million per year. One analysis, extrapolating from data from North Carolina, concluded that an estimated 829,000 illegal or self-induced abortions occurred in 1967." I am basing my comparison on the 829,000 figure in 1967 based on the study that extrapolated data from North Carolina. See Rachel Benson Gold, "Lessons Before *Roe*: Will Past Be Prologue?" *Guttmacher Report on Public Policy*, March 23, vol. 6, no. 1.

38. Laurie D. Elam-Evans, Lilo T. Strauss, Joy Herndon, Wilda Y. Parker, Sonya V. Bowens, Suzanne Zane, and Cynthia J. Berg, "Abortion Surveillance—United States 2000" (Atlanta, GA: Department of Health and Human Services Centers for Disease Control and Prevention, Nov. 28, 2003/52SS12; 1-32) table 2, http://www.cdc.gov/mmwr/preview/mmwrhtml/ss5212a1.htm.

39. The number of women ages 15–44 in 1967 was 40,387,00 and in 1997 it was 59,688,000. See Stephanie J. Ventura and Christine A. Bachrach, "Nonmarital Childbearing in the United States, 1940–1999" (Hyattsville, MD: National Center for Health Statistics, 2000), 32, http://www.cdc.gov/nchs/data/nvsr/nvsr48/nvs48_16.pdf.

40. Susan A. Cohen, "Envisioning Life Without *Roe:* Lessons Without Borders," *Guttmacher Report on Public Policy*, vol. 6, no. 2 (May 2003), http://www.guttmacher.org/pubs/tgr/06/2/gr060203.html.

unintended pregnancies end in induced abortion.[41] Of the roughly 6.3 million pregnancies a year in the United States, 50 percent are unintended. Half of these unintended pregnancies occur in 10 percent of women ages 15 through 44. This group of women tends to be teenagers and older married women who do not use birth control or only use it sporadically.[42] Tragically, 42 percent of all of these unintended pregnancies end in abortion—nearly 1.3 million abortions a year.[43]

In 1996, the Netherlands had an abortion rate of 6 abortions for every 1,000 women ages 15 through 44, while the United States had an abortion rate of 22 abortions for every 1,000 women in this age group.[44] The rather high rate of abortions in the United States compared to the Netherlands and other Western European countries is directly related to the relatively high number of unintended pregnancies.[45] The Netherlands has consistently had the lowest rate of unintended pregnancies in the world, and as a consequence it has consistently had the lowest abortion rate in the world.[46] An article in the journal *Patient Education and Counseling* argues that the Netherlands has a low abortion rate because of its family planning program, which "shows the following characteristics: a strong wish to reduce reliance on abortion, ongoing sexual and contraceptive education related to the actual experiences of the target groups, and low barrier family planning services."[47] It further states that in the Netherlands "acceptance of contraception preceded liberalization of abortion"[48] and that the "society accepts abortion only as a last resort."[49]

---

41. Cynthia Dailard, "Abortion in Context: United States and Worldwide."
42. Ibid.
43. Guttmacher Institute, "Get 'In the Know': 20 Questions about Pregnancy, Contraception, and Abortion," http://www.guttmacher.org/in-the-know/index.html (accessed May 30, 2007).
44. See Stanley K. Henshaw, Susheela Singh, and Taylor Haas, "Recent Trends in Abortion Rates Worldwide," *International Family Planning Perspectives*, vol. 25, no. 1 (March 1999), table 1, http://www.guttmacher.org/pubs/journals/2504499.html.
45. Cynthia Dailard, "Abortion in Context: United States and Worldwide."
46. Aida Torres, Elise F. Jones, "The Delivery of Family Planning Services in the Netherlands," *Family Planning Perspectives*, vol. 20, no. 2 (Mar.-Apr., 1988): 75–79. The low abortion rate in the Netherlands has been a subject of much study because since 1975, the Netherlands has had the lowest or one of the lowest abortion rates in the world. See Stanley K. Henshaw, Susheela Singh, and Taylor Haas, "Recent Trends in Abortion Rates Worldwide."
47. Evert Ketting, Adriaan P. Visser, "Contraception in the Netherlands: The low abortion rate explained," *Patient Education and Counseling*, vol. 23, no. 3 (July 1994): 161.
48. Ibid.
49. Ibid.

The importance of family planning services is also supported by data from the United States. According to the Guttmacher Institute research for the federal government, "publicly supported family planning services prevent some 1.3 million unintended pregnancies each year."[50] It is estimated that "if these unplanned pregnancies had occurred, they would have resulted in some 632,000 abortions, increasing the U.S. abortion rate by 40 percent."[51] Furthermore, "University of California researchers estimated that in 2002 alone, their state's effort to extend eligibility for Medicaid-subsidized family planning services to more lower-income women prevented 213,000 unintended pregnancies, averting 82,000 abortions."[52] In addition, an article in the *American Journal of Public Health* shows that 86 percent of the current decline in the pregnancy rate among teenagers in the United States is attributed to improved contraceptive use, while 14 percent is the result of abstinence.[53]

One of the clearest conclusions that can be drawn from social scientific data is that sex education with an emphasis on effective contraception is the best way to reduce the number of abortions. I am quite cognizant that this runs counter to Catholic teaching on contraception. I am simply filling out the social scientific portrait and the moral theologians, whom we have invited today, can sort this out. It is not my position to provide counsel on the choice we have in public life between the two evils of contraception and abortion. I would note, however, that serious moral choices are often choices between goods and evils. Sometimes the only right choice is the lesser of two evils.

This excursion into the subject of abortion was intended to show that each issue we are asked to consider is related to many other issues. Hence, isolating a particular issue to the detriment of the others is not a responsible way of engaging in public life. This could have been exemplified by taking any one of the fifty-plus issues the bishops ask us to consider and showing how it is related to a multitude of other issues. I chose abortion because I wanted to communicate quite clearly

50. Susan A. Cohen, "Toward Making Abortion 'Rare.'"
51. Ibid.
52. Ibid.
53. John S. Santelli, Laura Duberstein Lindberg, Lawrence B. Finer, and Susheela Singh, "Explaining Recent Declines in Adolescent Pregnancy in the United States: The Contribution of Abstinence and Improved Contraceptive Use," *American Journal of Public Health*, 97, no. 1 (January 2007): 150–156.

that by focusing on a host of issues today we are not turning a blind eye to abortion; indeed, we are engaging in a discussion that could ultimately help limit the number of abortions. The social scientific data on abortion corroborated my central point but also showed that when moral principles meet real life, there are many other issues that must be considered and that this presents us, as a pro-life community, with difficult choices.

Though we will always be faced with difficult choices, we can make a positive difference in American public life. We can do this not only in terms of voting, but also in many other ways. "Faithful Citizenship" lists several in encouraging Catholics to participate in public life "by working within political parties; by contributing money or time to campaigns; and by joining diocesan legislative networks, community organizations, and other efforts to apply Catholic principles in the public square."[54] Participating in the process is easier than ever before because of the Internet. Nonpartisan institutions are online and allow for easy access to data so that we can go beyond the pundits screaming at each other on CNN or Fox. Furthermore, the Internet provides access to our representatives and allows our voices to be heard. There are many recent examples of bad legislation being thwarted by public outcry through e-mails.

Our participation in public life inevitably will not be typified by "crystallized and consistently conservative political attitudes"[55] as evangelical Protestants. For, as "Faithful Citizenship" maintains,

> *The Catholic community enters public life not to impose sectarian doctrine but to act on our moral convictions, to share our experience in serving the poor and vulnerable, and to participate in the dialogue over our nation's future.*
>
> *A Catholic moral framework does not easily fit the ideologies of "right" or "left," nor the platforms of any party. Our values are often not "politically correct."*[56]

---

54. "Faithful Citizenship," 3.
55. Pew Research Center and Pew Forum, "Many Americans Uneasy With Mix of Religion and Politics," 3.
56. "Faithful Citizenship," 7.

> *Faithful citizenship calls Catholics to see civic and political responsibilities through the eyes of faith and to bring our moral convictions to public life. People of good will and sound faith can disagree about specific applications of Catholic principles. However, Catholics in public life have a particular responsibility to bring together consistently their faith, moral principles, and public responsibilities.*[57]

Let me conclude by repeating and completing a quotation from the Congregation of the Doctrine of the Faith that is cited in "Faithful Citizenship":

> *"The Christian faith is an integral unity, and thus it is incoherent to isolate some particular element to the detriment of the whole of Catholic doctrine. A political commitment to a single isolated aspect of the Church's social doctrine does not exhaust one's responsibility towards the common good." Decisions about candidates and choices about public policies require clear commitment to moral principles, careful discernment and prudential judgments based on the values of our faith.*[58]

Today, we have invited nationally recognized Catholic scholars to help us sort out Catholic moral principles and their application. The primary focus in the morning will be on moral principles and historical background, and in the afternoon the primary focus will be the application of these principles. The hope is that the talks and our discussion at the end of the day will help us carefully discern how to make prudential judgments "based on the values of our faith."[59]

---

57. Ibid., 3.
58. "Faithful Citizenship," 12. "Faithful Citizenship" is citing The Congregation for the Doctrine of the Faith, "Doctrinal Note on some questions regarding the participation of Catholics in political life," no. 4.
59. Ibid.

2. Fundamental Principles: Conscience, Religion, and Politics

Michael J. Himes, Boston College

My task at this conference is to lay out a few fundamental principles, which I shall do by concentrating on the meaning of three familiar words: *religion, politics,* and *conscience.* Everyone has some idea of what these terms mean. I shall try to make them seem strange again so that we can consider what they might mean.

Religion

What precisely do we mean by *religion?* At first, we might dismiss the question. Certainly we know what religion is. But think for a moment. Thomas Aquinas would have been very puzzled by the way most people use the term *religion* today. For example, he would have been astonished to find that some universities and colleges have departments of religious studies. This would have seemed exceedingly odd to Thomas because, prior to the eighteenth century, religion was the name of a particular virtue, like humility or prudence. Thus when Thomas wrote or spoke of religion, he meant a particular quality that was part of a virtuous life.[1] And what was that quality that was one characteristic of a virtuous life? It was awed respect before the presence of the Holy. That was what religion meant: awed respect for the Holy.

Consequently, Saint Thomas would have been surprised to hear people refer to the *Christian religion* or the *Muslim religion* or the *Jewish religion.* For Thomas that would have made no more sense than for someone to talk about the Christian humility or the Jewish humility or the Muslim humility, since both *religion* and *humility* were names of particular virtues.

Use of the term *religion* began to change in the eighteenth century. As people looked out over their world, they recognized that there were communities of people united by ways of thinking and acting that did not quite correspond to and were not accurately described by any of the terms that usually designated groups. These were communities that could not be called *nations* and were not properly described as *tribe* or

1. For example, *Summa theologicae* I-II, q. 60, a. 3; II-II, q. 81, a. 2, 3, 4, and numerous other citations.

families. So what word could be used to describe these groups of people who were united by certain sets of beliefs, certain styles of practice and of life, certain forms of prayer and worship? Gradually they came to be called *religions.* So we began to talk about *the* Christian religion, *the* Jewish religion, and so on, and often we today are unaware that this is a strange and relatively recent use of the word *religion.* Sometimes this distorts our understanding of what previous ages meant by the word. For example, one of the great works in the history of systematic theology is the book by John Calvin, the title of which is usually translated as *Institutes of the Christian Religion.* In fact, in Calvin's original Latin and French titles there is nothing corresponding to the word *the* in the English title. Calvin did not intend to write about the institutes or foundations that are the bases of the Christian religion as compared with the Buddhist religion or the Taoist religion. His purpose was to address the foundations of Christian religion, the foundations of the peculiarly Christian way of experiencing and expressing awed respect in the presence of the Holy, that is, Christian reverence for God. In the fashion typical before the eighteenth century, Calvin was not writing about the set of beliefs and practices that are hallmarks of a social group called *the Christian religion* but of the Christian way of practicing a particular virtue.

So what do we mean today by *religion* when we speak of religion and politics? I shall take an idea from the distinguished English Catholic theologian Nicholas Lash.[2] He suggests that what we mean when we talk about a religion, that is, when we use *religion* in its ordinary post–eighteenth-century meaning, might be described as a formation program—a program designed to form a particular kind of person. He mentions two essential elements in the religious formation of persons. (Please note that there may well be other elements, but certainly these two must be included. Observe also that Lash thinks that these two elements are necessary in any religious formation, not Christian formation alone.) The programs of personal and communal formation that we call religions are concerned with weaning us from idolatry and purifying our desires.[3] By weaning us from idolatry I mean educating

2. See Nicholas Lash, *The Beginning and the End of "Religion"* (Cambridge: Cambridge University Press, 1996), 3–25. I am selecting a few basic notions from Lash's rich and insightful discussion.
3. Lash, 19–22.

us to recognize that when we talk about God, we are talking about absolute Mystery.

The most important thing to know about Mystery is that, in the end, we do not know what we are talking about. That is why it is *Mystery.* The great temptation for all religious people—religious in the post–eighteenth-century sense of members of communal traditions that teach particular doctrines, inculcate particular ethical practices, and encourage particular styles of prayer and devotion—is to claim that we believe in God who is absolute Mystery and then to chatter on like we know what we are talking about.

The most basic thing that we must recognize about God is that God transcends all our categories and images for thinking about God. Whatever goes on in your head when you hear the word *God* is not God. It may be a very good image or concept, biblically based, rooted in doctrine, magisterially approved, traditionally used, but it is *not* God. Only God is God, and God is greater than our best image or concept of God. That is the point of the first commandment: Make no image of God.

When I was growing up in Brooklyn, I used to think that at least one of the Ten Commandments, the first, was not a big problem. If making images of God—idolatry—meant sacrificing to false gods, very little of it was going on in Brooklyn as far as I could see. No one that I knew of in my neighborhood cut up oxen for Zeus or slew the odd goat for Odin. We seemed to have succeeded with the first commandment. In fact, the reason that the first commandment is the first is that it is the besetting sin of religious people. We all set up images of God and need to be constantly reminded that, however rich, deep, consoling, however biblically based and doctrinally rooted, they remain *images.* We must remember that God transcends our *best* image of God.

We must be formed to recognize that we cannot "box" God, define God, establish limits to how God acts, what God wills, and how God deals with us. God remains sovereignly Mystery. This does not mean that we know nothing true about God. Indeed we do! But we do not possess the truth absolutely. Only God knows God absolutely. This is why the Hebrew Scriptures insist that we must not make an image of God. Only God can make an image of God, and God has done so. According to Genesis 1:26–27, you and I are made in the image of God. We do not need to fashion an image of God because God has fashioned us as God's image. Look at your neighbor; look in the mirror. That is where the true image and likeness of God is to be found. So the first formative task of a truly religious tradition is to educate us to acknowledge that God is always sovereignly Mystery.

The second task of religious formation is to purify our desires. One of the many things I have learned from Saint Augustine is that, in attempting to understand any person or community, the most important question to ask is, "What do you love?" This is not at all the same as asking what amuses someone, or gives him or her pleasure, or what a person has a taste for. The question is, "What do you deeply, passionately, centrally desire?" Know that and you know the person or the community. What is it that makes someone "tick"? What do you really love? What are you really hungry for? What is it that gets you out of bed every morning? What is it that you really want?

To be able to recognize what we truly desire and then to purify that desire, to sharpen it, hone it, make it keener and evermore pressing—that is what a religion does. A religion is a formation program designed to wean us from idolatry—to make us evermore conscious that we stand before Mystery—and to purify our desires—to enable us to feel evermore keenly our desire for what we love at the core of our being, what Augustine famously wrote that the heart is restless for.[4]

Politics

Often I find that, in trying to introduce students to texts from the classical world, such as the Fathers of the Church, a problem many of the students have is that words that the ancient world found immensely powerful, positive, and evocative actually have negative connotations today. *Rhetoric* is an example. To help students to understand why rhetoric was a central element, indeed in many ways *the* central element, in classical education, is very difficult, because for most modern Americans *rhetoric* means elaborate, confusing, and probably deliberately misleading language. To say that something was "a lot of rhetoric" means that it had no substance and, indeed, may be deceptive. Rhetoric has been debased to mean the stock-in-trade of Madison Avenue. What was an enormously positive word for the ancient world has come to mean little more than "advertising." And much the same process

4. Augustine, *Confessions* I, 1.

of debasement is true of the word *politics*. For many contemporary Americans, to say that someone acted politically means craftily, slyly, possibly deceptively, underhandedly, sneakily, "behind one's back." Today, alas, *politics* names a necessary but all too often sleazy aspect of a community's life.

In the ancient world, *politics* was a word that carried very positive meaning. Indeed, for Aristotle it was the crown of philosophy, the field of thought and action to which all other studies led. When one had studied all the other fields of philosophy, then one was ready to turn one's attention to politics.[5] For Aristotle, as indeed for many classical thinkers, politics is the study of how to organize communities in order to make the good life possible for their members—all sorts of communities, not just cities or states or nations, but marriages, families, circles of friends, schools, businesses, and we might add parishes and dioceses. How does one organize a community in such a way that a genuinely good life is fostered for the members of that community? Politics is about enabling people to live good lives. And what is the good life? The good life, according to Aristotle, is one in which a human being exercises his or her talents, powers, and capacities to the full in an endeavor worthy of human beings. This, of course, entailed—and here one can see why politics was the summation of all philosophy—that a good politician was someone who knew what it is to be a human being and what goals were worthy of a human being. If you were engaged in shaping a true community, you had to understand what a human being can and ought to be and what kinds of activities and goals are worthy of that kind of a human being. To be a politician was to be a philosopher.

How do *religion* (in the sense that I have suggested) and *politics* (in its classical meaning) relate to one another? In answering that question I must first make a distinction that is both simple and important, namely, that there is a difference between talking about religion and politics and talking about church and state. Church and state are the

5. For example, *Politics I*, 1, Jonathan Barnes, ed., *The Complete Works of Aristotle: The Revised Oxford Translation*, 2 vols. (Princeton: Princeton University Press, 1984), 2:1986: "Every state is a community of some kind, and every community is established with a view to some good; for everyone always acts in order to obtain that which they think good. But, if all communities aim at some good, the state or political community, which is the highest of all, and which embraces all the rest, aims at good in a greater degree than any other, and at the highest good."

names of two kinds of institutions, and I think the experience of the United States over the past two centuries has amply demonstrated that for the well-being and health of both institutions they can and should be kept separate. Religion and politics, on the other hand, are not the names of institutions. Rather, they are aspects of human experience, and if one tries to separate them, one produces fragmented human beings. Religion and politics cannot be separated because human beings cannot be divided into isolated segments. So it is perfectly possible to champion the separation of church and state without in any way advocating the separation of religion and politics. The first fosters the health of both organizations; the latter is impossible and the attempt is ultimately destructive of human life.

If religion and politics cannot be separated, how are they related?

Forty years ago the distinguished American sociologist Robert Bellah published an essay, "Civil Religion in America," which created a furor and ignited a flurry of publications debating his contentions.[6] Some critics became terribly exercised about the notion of a civil religion in America because they took the phrase *civil religion* to mean that Americans worshiped America, that America became the religious ideal, the "god" of Americans. Bellah repeatedly explained that this was not what he intended by the phrase. By *American civil religion* he did not mean some sort of American Shintoism. He was not suggesting that America was itself a religion. His purpose was to point to a religious element that is foundational to American self-understanding.

Although we may be a society that has advocated and celebrated the separation of church and state, we have never been a society that has separated religion and politics. In fact, the origins of the American republic are deeply rooted in religious tradition, the most obvious and most often mentioned being the tradition of New England Puritanism. What was distinctive and, in Bellah's opinion, especially wonderful about the religious dimension in American life was precisely that the nation did not set itself up as the object of its own worship, as that holy reality before which it stands in awe. Instead, fundamental

6. Originally published in *Dædalus* 96:1 (Winter, 1967): 1–21, it was republished in Robert N. Bellah, *Beyond Belief: Essays on Religion in a Post-Traditional World* (New York: Harper and Row, 1970), 168–189, and more recently in Robert N. Bellah and Steven M. Tipton, eds., *The Robert Bellah Reader* (Durham, NC: Duke University Press, 2006), 225–245.

to American self-understanding is the claim that there is an object of worship, the Holy before which one stands awestruck and that it transcends the nation.

The classic statement of this claim is the opening of the Declaration of Independence: "We hold these truths to be self-evident, that all men are created equal, that they are endowed by their Creator with certain inalienable Rights, that among these are Life, Liberty and the pursuit of Happiness." Please notice that the declaration is not that all Americans are created equal, or that all citizens of the United States are endowed with certain inalienable rights, but rather that all human beings, the vast majority of whom are not citizens of the United States, have rights given them by their Creator. It is that these rights are intrinsic, not in being an American citizen but in being a human being, that central to American life is a claim about the relationship of the Creator to all people. This claim provides the deep religious foundation for American life and experience. Our national life and community are grounded, not in a declaration of the rights of citizens, but in a declaration of the rights of human beings. On that foundation, quite properly described as religious, we organize ourselves a community, the task of politics. Consequently religion and politics can never be separated. If one is engaged in political life, one has some notion, however undeveloped, of what a genuinely good life for human beings is. We may never have thought about it carefully, may never have worked through its implications. But necessarily we bring to public life and political decision-making some notion of what a human being is and ought to be and how a human being can and ought to act. Because of that often implicit understanding, we decide that certain things ought or ought not to be done in our society, that our community should be organized in this fashion and must not be organized in that fashion.

We all bring to our public and political lives some stance toward what is truly good. Sometimes those stances are admirable, sometimes deplorable. Inevitably they lead us back to the purifying of our desires, the clarifying of what we really love. Some people may be convinced that what is truly good is their prosperity and therefore make their political decisions in view of what they think will foster that prosperity. Some may be thoroughly Machiavellian in their conviction that the true good, what they really love, is gaining and expanding power. For some being elected is the truly good, and they will accordingly say and do anything to get elected. People's notion of the truly good may be woefully inadequate, destructively selfish, but they operate nonetheless with some notion of the good. That is why clarifying and purifying what we really love is one of the tasks of personal formation or, as I have suggested, religion. And this is why it can never be separated from politics.[7]

Conscience

What has this to do with conscience? Well, let me suggest to you that we start by looking at the root meaning of the word. The word *conscience* comes from the Latin *conscientia*, literally, "knowing together with." I suggest that we might helpfully examine that notion of "knowing together with" in two senses. The first is that really knowing something requires that we know *that* thing in relation to *everything* we know. Knowing means being able to put things together, seeing how the things we know fit. When we know something as true we contextualize it, that is, we incorporate it into the nexus of everything else we hold as true. But there is a second sense of "knowing together with." We know and acknowledge what we know to be true with other knowers. We never know something as an isolated individual; we always know as a member of the community of knowers. By being part of a community, by exchanging ideas, by arguing and debating and working with others, we grow in both the breadth and depth of knowledge, we know more and we know that we know. Both these senses of "knowing together with," of *conscientia*—that we know by incorporating new knowledge into the whole of our prior knowledge and that we know as a member of a community of knowers—give us insight into the meaning of *conscience.*

The worst distortion of the notion of conscience in the twentieth

---

7. The classic statement of this is in Book 19 of Augustine, *The City of God Against the Pagans*, ed. and trans. by R. W. Dyson (Cambridge: Cambridge University Press, 1998), 960: "But let us disregard this definition of a people and adopt another: let us say that a 'people' is an assembled multitude of rational creatures bound together by a common agreement as to the objects of their love. In this case, if we are to discover the character of any people, we have only to examine what it loves. If it is an assembled multitude, not of animals but of rational creatures, and is united by a common agreement as to what it loves, then it is not absurd to call it a 'people,' no matter what the objects of its love may be. Clearly, however, the better the objects of this agreement, the better the people; and the worse the objects, the worse the people."

century stems from the Walt Disney film, *Pinocchio.* When they hear the word *conscience,* many people think of Jiminy Cricket. The popular image of one's conscience is a little figure (angel or demon or, if you are partial to insects, Jiminy Cricket) who sits on one's shoulder and whispers in one's ear, "Don't do that. You ought to do this." Pleasant as it might be if we had such a constant counselor, this image is not at all what the Catholic Christian moral tradition means by conscience.

Conscience is not a small external voice advising or warning or threatening us. Conscience is a "knowing with"; it is a holding together of all the things we know and believe and a fruit of one's participation in community. Conscience is not about knowing what is right and wrong in a particular situation. It is not the application of a set of guidelines or rules given us by parents, government, or church or of a natural law written in our hearts by God. Such laws or guidelines and knowing how to interpret and apply them to concrete situations are not unimportant in human life, but they are not central to what our tradition has meant by conscience. What is central to conscience is the integration of everything we know and believe about ourselves as human beings, about the people around us as human beings, and about the world in which we find ourselves, in a coherent whole in which our decisions and actions fit. It is like what has already been said about politics. To act politically one must know what it is to be a human being and what a good life for a human being would be. In order to act with a well-formed conscience, you must know who you are, who those around you are, what your world is like, and how your actions, your words, your ways of doing or not doing fit or fail to fit with that understanding of yourself and others and the world in which we all find ourselves.

One of the most important qualities of a human being, perhaps the most important, is integrity. I do not mean honesty, although that is certainly a part of what I mean by integrity. Nor do I mean keeping one's word and being faithful to one's commitments, although that too is certainly part of integrity. First of all, *integrity* means being an integer, being a whole, being one complete reality. Imagine all your family, friends, colleagues, associates, neighbors assembled at your funeral. All the people gathered around your coffin should be able to recognize one another's description of you. When your son or daughter speaks of you to your business associate, when your business partner speaks of you to your physician, when your physician speaks of you to your pastor, and your pastor to your next-door neighbor, and your next-door neighbor to your attorney, and your attorney to your closest friend, and your friend to your spouse, they should all know that they are speaking of the same person.

We should not be a collection of separate facets or a series of different roles. Who one is in his or her family is who one is in his or her profession, and that is who one is with one's friends and in the voting booth and at prayer. All the parts fit together as a single human being, an integer, a whole person.

The test of integrity is the capacity to be a whole person in such a way that all the many acts and choices in our life fit together so that all who knew us in all our different roles know that they were in touch with the same person. Integrity is both the root of a good conscience and the fruit of a good conscience. To be a person of integrity is to recognize who I am. It is to be clear and single-hearted about what I love, what I truly desire, what I hold as truly good, to attend carefully to the ways I must act in response to that good. It is to reflect on how my actions affect those around me, how I might be able to help others to discover that good in their lives, and how I may cooperate in organizing the communities in which I dwell so that I and others may come to that good in our lives. That is the root and fruit of conscience.

Certainly conscience involves practical decision-making. Practical, concrete decisions, however, are always made within a very broad horizon. If this is what it is to be a human being, and if this is what I love, and this is what I believe to be true of others, and this is what a good community would look like, how can I act to make this real for myself and others in the concrete situation in which I find myself and under the practical conditions with which I must deal? Thus the first aspect of conscience, this "knowing together with," is the ability to hold together all that we know and believe in a coherent whole so that we do not become fragmented persons. We must act with integrity and for integrity, not as disintegrated persons. This is the first aspect of conscience.

The second aspect of conscience is a knowing together with others. No one forms his or her conscience in isolation. We always form our understandings of who we are, what a human being is, and what a good life for a human being is, in conversation with others. One problem I find in introducing contemporary students to classical texts is that words that once carried powerful positive meanings for the ancient world now convey negative meanings, such as, for *rhetoric* and *politics.* A second problem has to do with the status and meaning of community. Students are deeply shaped by our culture to assume that individuals matter and communities are at best helpful supports for individuals and at worst oppressive obstacles for individuals. But communities are always secondary to the individual. That was certainly not the assumption of the Greek and Roman world.

One way I invite students to think about this cultural assumption is to reflect on Plato's depiction of Socrates, unjustly condemned to death by the Athenians because the kind of life and teaching he has offered have been a reproach to and criticism of their values. Socrates could have argued, perhaps successfully, to be sentenced to exile rather than death, but he chose not to do so. Even as the day of his execution drew near, some of his disciples arranged for him to escape from Athens and go into voluntary exile. But Socrates refused because exile would be far worse than death. Much better to drink the hemlock than to go into exile. To most young American students that is utterly incomprehensible. After all, Socrates is offered, in effect, a pleasant retirement in a nice resort community. What is so bad about that?

Why did Socrates choose death rather than exile, and why did such a choice seem perfectly sensible and right to the ancient world? Socrates and the classical culture that he shaped and by which he was shaped took it as self-evident that one cannot be a truly human being in isolation. Intrinsic to being a full human being is the capacity to take part in a community. Socrates' community was Athens. If he left it to dwell in another city where he was not a citizen, he might live in a very comfortable private retirement but he would not be able to participate in public life and so would not live a fully human life. Better death than that kind of disintegration as a human being.

It is very hard for young American students (and perhaps older Americans as well) to appreciate such a perspective. We think of ourselves first as individuals, and often "individual" is synonymous with "isolated." In fact, we become who we are only because of interactions—some positive, some negative, some wonderfully pleasant, some terribly painful—with other human beings throughout our lives.

We are the products of our families; our neighborhoods; our

circles of friends, of our teachers and of pastors; of the authors we have read and the music we have sung and the paintings we have enjoyed; of the films we have seen and the plays we have attended; and of the laws under which we live and the legislators who have enacted them and the citizens who elected those legislators. We are products of all our relationships, proximate and remote (although in today's shrinking world of rapid transportation and instantaneous communication, few relationships are all that remote). So if we are to be fully formed human beings with well-formed consciences, we form our consciences only by interaction with others—only by conversation, by discussion, by instruction and questioning, by debate, by willingness to be taught and sometimes by courage to reject. Our consciences, like the whole of our individuality, are always dependent on our communities, which is why you must belong to a community in order to have a fully formed conscience and why it must be a truly good community if you are to have a rightly formed conscience.

As the community forms our conscience along with us, simultaneously our actions as conscientious members of the community shape the community. Our community and our conscience are always shaping one another. That's why I will never be a fully formed human being with a fully and rightly formed conscience—I will never be the Michael Himes that God envisions and calls me to be—until all of the communities I inhabit are the family, friends, nation, church, and world that God envisions and calls them to be. My conscience will only be well formed to the extent that I help you to have a well-formed conscience, and your conscience will only be well formed to the extent that you help me to have a well-formed conscience. We are in this together. To know that is to be awed by the responsibility we have for one another's well-being. It is religious. To know that is also to find ourselves enmeshed in community. It is political. We must work together for our individual and communal good, and we must demand that the leaders of our various communities be people whose consciences are well and truly formed.

On that note, I conclude with a quotation from one of the most perceptive thinkers about conscience and politics in the last 300 years, Edmund Burke, the great Irish member of the English Parliament in the late eighteenth century. It is from a speech he gave in 1774 during his election campaign in Bristol, the borough he represented in parliament. After thanking the electors of Bristol who had voted for him, he said:

> *Certainly, gentlemen, it ought to be the happiness and glory of a representative to live in the strictest union, the closest correspondence, and the most unreserved communication with his constituents. Their wishes ought to have great weight with him; their opinion, high respect; their business, unremitted attention. It is his duty to sacrifice his repose, his pleasures, his satisfactions, to theirs—and above all, ever, and in all cases, to prefer their interest to his own. But his unbiased opinion, his mature judgment, his enlightened conscience, he ought not to sacrifice to you, to any man, or to any set of men living. These he does not derive from your pleasure, no, nor from the law and the constitution. They are a trust from Providence, for the abuse of which he is deeply answerable. Your representative owes you, not his industry only, but his judgment; and he betrays, instead of serving you, if he sacrifices it to your opinion.*[8]

Would that we had more Edmund Burkes! But then we would also need more voters like those of Bristol.

8. Edmund Burke, "Speech at the Conclusion of the Poll in Bristol, November 3, 1774," in Robert A. Smith, ed., *Edmund Burke on Revolution* (New York: Harper and Row, 1968), 52.

3. Catholics and American Politics: A Historical Perspective

David J. O'Brien, Ph.D., Loyola Professor of Roman Catholic Studies, College of the Holy Cross

During the 2004 Presidential campaign the Catholic question was back, but in an entirely new form. For John F. Kennedy in 1960 the Catholic question was about overcoming America's deeply rooted suspicion of Catholics.[1] In 2004 the question for presidential nominee Senator John F. Kerry was not whether he would be accepted by non-Catholics but whether he would be denied Communion by a Catholic priest. In 2003 the Vatican had encouraged bishops to call pro-choice Catholics to account and one bishop, Raymond L. Burke of La Crosse, Wisconsin, denied Communion to a prominent Catholic politician, Congressman David Obey, drawing intense media interest.[2] Meeting in Denver in June, the bishops decided to leave the Communion decision up to each bishop. Most simply scolded pro-choice Catholic politicians, but several insisted that priests should refuse to offer Kerry Communion. A Kerry staff person had the job of finding a church each Sunday where the candidate could be sure that would not happen.

Democrats, not Republicans, absorbed these well-publicized shots, and Kerry and his party never figured out how to deal with their Catholic question. The Republican Party, in contrast, made an unprecedented bid for Catholic votes. Advised by smart Catholic conservatives, President

---

1. Thomas Carty, *A Catholic in the White House: Religion, Politics and John F. Kennedy's Presidential Campaign* (New York: Palgrave Macmillan, 2004).

2. The incident is relevant to this text. Obey said that he was a "John Courtney Murray kind of Catholic, Archbishop Burke is not." Obey thought they differed over very little, most significantly about the "requirements the law can be expected to impose in a democratic society on those who do not share our religious beliefs." Obey would not have laws that "would be unenforceable and would tear this society apart. That is my judgment to make and I am the one obligated to make it." Archbishop Burke, as a churchman, argued that the moral question was one for the hierarchy to make and on fundamental issues such as abortion Catholics were expected to abide by their judgment. See David R. Obey, "My Conscience, My Vote," *America* 191, no. 4 (August 16, 2004), and Archbishop Raymond L. Burke, "Prophecy for Justice: Catholic Politicians and Bishops," *America* 190, no. 20 (June 21, 2004). Archbishop Burke wrote a pastoral letter on the subject of politics soon after he became archbishop of St. Louis: "Catholics and Political Responsibility," *Origins* 33 (January 29, 2004): 557.

Bush, with the help of Richard Neuhaus, editor of *First Things*, a friend Bush called "Father Richard," mastered Catholic-friendly "culture of life" and "compassionate conservative" language.[3] The GOP also built its Catholic (and other religious outreach) strategies around evidence that Catholics who went to church regularly were apt to vote Republican ("good" Catholics vote Republican, "bad" Catholics Democrat). The party developed a superb organization for reaching Catholic voters in key states and raising suspicion everywhere about Kerry's Catholic fidelity. Independent Catholic groups assisted, blanketing the country with the message that "nonnegotiable" issues of human life should define Catholic political responsibility. The bishops issued their usual nonpartisan voter guide, "Faithful Citizenship," in which they gave clear priority to abortion but did so amid a broad range of peace and social justice issues that also merited consideration.[4] Unfortunately, given the heat of partisan conflict, the American Church's silence on the Iraq war, and a remarkable decline in public advocacy of the consistent ethic of life, the bishops' text seemed indecisive, and it was widely ignored.[5]

So the 2004 campaign was marked by unprecedented attention to the Catholic vote and by equally unprecedented attention to the relationship between Catholic politicians and their bishops. In the election's aftermath, and in 2006, it was evident that interest in "religion and politics" remained intense, that Catholics constituted a crucially important swing vote, and that the politics of American Catholicism—its internal relationships and external engagements—

---

3. These quotes are from a *New York Times* account of a meeting of President Bush with religious leaders May 31, 2004.

4. The bishops helpfully collected their 2004 statement along with Vatican texts and subsequent committee reports into one volume, *Catholics and Political Life* (Washington, DC, 2004).

5. The bishops' statement and follow-up in midsummer of 2004 received minimal media attention, a problem complicated by Senator Kerry's failure to recognize its presence or develop a comprehensive response to challenges to his position on what GOP Catholics and the media consistently identified as definitive Catholic issues. Catholic leaders sympathetic to the comprehensive position of "Faithful Citizenship" were all but invisible, leaving it to several groups of younger, less experienced Catholic laypeople to develop Web sites and media strategies to reach Catholic voters with the bishops' message. After the election these groups coalesced into a new organization, Catholics in Alliance for the Common Good.

would be an important factor in determining the nation's future.[6] I want to concentrate today on one of the most important features of this recent history: the absence of organized Catholic support for the position represented by "Faithful Citizenship."

Obviously Catholics have become steadily more independent, and more politically divided, in their voting in recent years, but the basic patterns of social thought and action have remained fairly consistent.[7] At least since the 1890s Catholics and their bishops have usually been progressive on economic issues, conservative on cultural issues, and divided on foreign policy. Similarly, they have always had to combine (1) affirmative participation in the politics of a democratic and religiously pluralist society, with emphasis on the public interest and the common good; (2) protection of their own, sometimes-endangered distinctive interests, including moral interests, such as Catholic education and exemption from requirements contrary to Church teaching, such as provision of abortion in Catholic medical facilities, requiring organized advocacy and lobbying; and (3) prophetic witness to essential values, such as "the protection of human life from conception to natural death." The first responsibility requires emphasis on shared responsibility as American citizens. When we meet at city hall or enter the voting booth, Catholics draw on common civic experiences and shared values to implement what they hope will be the common good, and they regard it as a genuine good, independent of the good of their church. The interest group model extends beyond protecting the freedom of religious, educational, and charitable institutions. Immigrant Catholics learned that their interests as ethnic groups and as wage workers required self-interest organizations, trade unions, political machines, ethnic associations. At times, this produces a form of identity politics, when civic action united Catholics and clarifies boundaries between Catholics and others. That once was the function of the school question,

6. One of the best papers is William A. Galston, "Religion, Moral Values and the Democratic Party" (May 2006) available on the Web site of the Pew Forum on Religion and Public Life (http://pewforum.org/events/?EventID=115). For a somewhat different view, see William V. D'Antonio, James D. Davidson, Dean R. Hoge, and Mary L. Gautier, *American Catholics Today: New Realities of Their Faith and Their Church* (Lanham, MD: Rowman & Littlefield, 2007), chapter 7. Also see Clarke E. Cochran and David C. Cochran, *The Catholic Vote: A Guide for the Perplexed* (Maryknoll, NY: Orbis, 2007).

7. George J. Marlin and Michael Barone, *The American Catholic Voter: Two Hundred Years of Political Impact* (South Bend, IN: St. Augustine's Press, 2004).

pro-family campaigns against birth control and dirty movies, and regular protests against secularism and liberalism. The prophetic style arises from impatience with the compromises required by civic engagement and the self-centered acquisition of power required by interest group politics and opts for a more evangelical approach, a Catholic version of the Protestant social gospel. Here citizens and communities make a direct move from moral prescription to public action with little reference to negotiation or mobilization, taking a stand on issues regarded as "fundamental" to personal or community integrity. Faith commitment, in this case, requires a discipleship that places Christian commitments beyond the claims of citizenship and group self-interest.[8]

My book *Public Catholicism* attempts to locate these "styles" in the social history of American Catholics. The Republican approach was evident as early as John and Charles Carroll, and it found a seemingly secure home in the aspiring Catholic middle class of the twentieth century. Interest group politics found its source in the experience of urban, ethnic, working-class Catholics and in the concrete needs of the institutional Church. Its staying power is associated with persistent bottom-up community building and ever-renewed concerns about the unity, identity, integrity, and independence of the Church. The evangelical style is the sharp end of identity politics, demanding discipleship, devaluing citizenship, and practicing, when serious, what Max Weber called a "politics of ultimate ends."[9] In its explosive form evangelical faith has fueled innumerable reform movements in American history, but in its softer forms it often falls prey to American individualism, innocence, and moral sentimentality. As Catholic subcultures continue to erode, we can expect the further spread of evangelical attitudes among American Catholics.

Most of the time religious believers in our free society prefer the Republican "community of conscience" model of religion and politics. Each of us forms our conscience in a community of distinctive belief; we then carry our beliefs into action in the marketplace and the public square. There we try our best to live according to our beliefs and, when serious public issues arise, we try to persuade others of the wisdom of

---

8. Since these three "styles" or impulses became clear in debates surrounding the 1980s' pastoral letters on nuclear weapons and on the American economy, I have made this argument in numerous papers and in the concluding section of *Public Catholicism: American Catholics and Public Life, 1786–1986* (New York: Macmillan, 1988).
9. Max Weber, "Politics as a Vocation" (pamphlet), Philadelphia, 2000.

our position, using language and moral norms we hold in common, such as civil rights and the public interest. We argue that Catholic schools and hospitals serve the public interest, that abortion contradicts American values of human dignity, not just Catholic teachings about conception. We bring our lay experience back to church, to challenge the community to avoid sectarianism and separatism and stake its shared civic responsibilities with moral seriousness. At our best, we nourish persons with strong convictions, compassionate hearts, and civic intelligence, and we hope to provide community support to help people from our community live with genuine integrity, that is with a fairly close relationship between their beliefs and their actions.

Catholics value conscience, as do all Americans, but Catholics also have a strong doctrine of Church, and that has never been an easy sell in American religious culture. Catholics are expected to pay attention to Church teaching and to the community's collective experience as they form their conscience. Bishops are ordained to promote the unity and the integrity of the community of faith. In some societies, bishops could call on the state to help them, a practice that left behind some rather undemocratic habits. Across the world Catholics were reluctant to give up on the Catholic state, but in the United States bishops understood from the start that coercion was not an option. People would make up their own minds, so clergy would have to carry out their responsibilities through invitation and persuasion. Still, they were Catholics, not Congregationalists, so there were moments when they spoke with authority on behalf of the whole community, and sometimes they called people to account, as when the bishop excommunicated some lay leaders who resisted racial integration in Louisiana in the 1960s. In 1983, the American bishops condemned the use of strategic nuclear weapons and touched the limits of "community of conscience" as they came very close to requiring Catholics to abandon military or industrial posts too close to the nuclear button. But as good Americans they were attentive to the public interest, respectful toward their people, and cautious in their judgments.[10]

10. See "The Challenge of Peace: God's Promise and Our Response" (Washington, DC: USCCB, 1983), the most influential pastoral letter ever published by the United States Catholic Bishops. In it the bishops speak of two styles of teaching: one for dialogue among Christians, the other for dialogue with fellow citizens, both in considerable tension with the prophetic stance arising from the conflict between the way of the gospel and the awesome power of nuclear weapons. Discussion of Catholic political responsibility could well begin with consideration of this letter and the moral questions it engages so honestly.

The American democratic experience suggests that, at least on matters that touch public life, Catholics must look not only to the teaching of the Church and the demands of the gospel but to the needs and norms of the civil community. To be the Church, with integrity and fidelity, in a free and religiously pluralistic society, is a matter of shared civic responsibility. As Father Bryan Hehir often says, the Church has no political agenda of its own but it seeks to defend human life, support human rights, and strengthen the unity of the human family. This stance received reinforcement in the teachings of the Second Vatican Council, which were proclaimed during the 1960s, as Americans wrestled with bitter conflicts over race, poverty, the Vietnam War, and abortion. As the hierarchy attempted to assist in the development of what theologian John Courtney Murray called the public moral consensus on the basis of which citizens and policymakers respond to public problems, differences of approach and emphasis naturally appeared. In 1976 a team of bishops led by Cardinal Cooke of New York visited with presidential candidates Jimmy Carter and incumbent Gerald Ford. They emerged from the meeting with Carter to tell the press they were "disappointed" with his position on abortion. Their word was "encouraged" after the Ford visit. The difference attracted considerable media attention and the implied preference disturbed their fellow bishops. The Bishops' Administrative Committee, under the leadership of then-Archbishop Joseph Bernardin, quickly produced a short pamphlet entitled "Political Responsibility in an Election Year." It laid out Church teaching on civic responsibility and the principles that should guide the formation of conscience, then concluded with a list of issues on which the bishops had taken a position, arranged in alphabetical order with abortion first. The list was long, reflecting the recent policy activism of the bishops' conference. This 1976 statement launched a tradition, as the bishops offered similar pastoral statements every four years, most recently "Faithful Citizenship" in 2003. The next edition is under construction behind the shrinking walls of the downsized national bishops' conference in Washington.

Several things can be said about these statements. First, as was evident to all in 2004, they did not end the tensions within the bishops' conference over the priority that should be assigned to abortion. Every election cycle, some bishops would comment that a candidate's position on that question required special consideration, even more if that candidate was a Catholic. You need only recall 1984 when New

York's John Cardinal O'Connor became embroiled in a well-publicized argument over abortion politics with Governor Mario Cuomo, then attacked Vice Presidential candidate Geraldine Ferraro, both New York–area Catholics. Bernardin's "consistent ethic of life" emerged from these differences. It was a noble effort to unite the hierarchy and lend coherence and depth to the broad agenda of justice and peace issues that engaged the bishops. Their engagement with these issues was less political than pastoral, some connected to their local work in education, social services, and civil rights, some connected with problems of poverty, violence, and human rights brought to their attention by sister churches, missionary orders, and the Vatican.

But Bernardin's comprehensive approach has always been challenged. When John Paul II became pope and appointed pro-life priority bishops to key sees, the balance began to shift, leading to further internal debates, to Bernardin's ill-fated common ground initiative, and to the relocation of the consistent ethic position and its advocates like Cardinal Bernardin and Father Hehir from the center to the left of American Catholic politics, a process treated ever so gingerly by Peter Steinfels in his account of this period.[11]

Second, this election-year approach was closely connected with the pastoral letters on nuclear weapons and the economy of the 1980s. Indeed the 1983 peace pastoral, with its striking differences between the near nonviolence of its theological sections and the Jesus-free analysis of nuclear policy, almost perfectly illustrated the Republican position. In the letter the bishops themselves referred to two styles of teaching—one appropriate for church basements, another for conversations at the Pentagon. What made it so significant was that it emerged from lengthy dialogue within and beyond the community of faith, that it was almost unanimously approved by an already divided hierarchy, and that its tensions accurately reflected the actual experience of the vast majority of lay Catholics and the bishops themselves. All of us use two languages, complete with distinct symbols and emotional repertoires—one for faith, family, and friends; another for workplace and the not-so-naked public square. The possibilities, and tensions, of that "citizen of two cities" position have been and remain at the very

11. Peter Steinfels, *A People Adrift: The Crisis of the Roman Catholic Church in America* (New York: Simon & Schuster, 2003).

center of the American and/or Catholic question that lies at the heart of contemporary American Catholic controversy.

Third, with the political responsibility statements like "Faithful Citizenship," and with the pastoral letters, there was an implementation problem. To accompany their election-year statements the bishops prepared educational materials for use by local bishops and some dioceses organized public forums, legislative networks, and statewide multi-issue lobbying organizations, but awareness of Catholic social teaching and Catholic issue advocacy remained uneven. Catholics generally backed the broad positions taken by the bishops on almost all issues except capital punishment, but they were far more aware of the clear moral position on abortion than they were of specific stands on other questions. So-called pro-life Catholic groups were active in and out of the church, but "seamless garment" advocates and lay Catholics with nuanced positions on this complex question almost never opened dialogue with Catholic politicians and more or less avoided the issues in parishes and classrooms. This public emphasis on abortion was reflected in the climate of internal Church politics, which was supportive of abortion prioritization as leaders moved from the Bernardin-era emphasis on shared responsibility for civic life to a John Paul II–era emphasis on the identity and integrity of the Catholic community.

As one example, in 2000 Worcester Bishop Daniel P. Reilly, a Bernardin ally, under intense pressure from the pro-life movement, at the last minute forced the state Democratic Party to move a scheduled rally from a rented Church facility because most statewide candidates were both Catholic and pro-choice. Just a week later the diocese sponsored a daylong workshop in the same hall designed to help local teachers, pastoral ministers, and priests use that year's version on "Faithful Citizenship." The bishop's staff, in the bishop's name, did massive direct mail, newsletter, and telephone invitations; they had an impressive array of speakers headed by John Carr, head of the Department of Social Development and World Peace at the bishops' conference in Washington; but, aside from speakers, the bishop and his director of the social justice office, fewer than a dozen people showed up. In retrospect, the absence in 2004 of effective organized support for the Bernardin-Hehir stance of "Faithful Citizenship" was unfortunate but predictable.

Fourth, the political responsibility statements and the 1980s pastoral letters were tied to an ecclesiology of shared political responsibility.

The intense problems of racism, urban violence, and war in the 1960s forced acknowledgment that Catholics shared with others responsibility to clarify the moral issues at stake and find constructive solutions to urgent and critical problems. This led to ecumenical coalitions, priests and nuns on other people's picket lines, and unprecedented and very serious divisions in the Catholic community. Even the most conservative bishops understood that when they spoke and acted on such issues, they needed the support of their people and priests. Many embarked on deliberate, well-funded, educational and pastoral initiatives on racism and social justice and later on abortion. Some among the leaders thought more was needed to build collaboration among bishops, priests, religious, and laypeople in order to carry out the social mission of the Church. That is what the 1976 Call to Action project was all about.

The bishops' 1974–1976 bicentennial program that climaxed with the first national convention of the American Catholic Church was designed to unite the Church for mission, now understood in John XXIII terms as a shared quest for peace, justice, and human rights. At that conference Cardinal Dearden spelled out the work of incorporating new understandings of public responsibility into procedures and programs for the Church:

> *All of us are against racism and war and hypocrisy and violence. All of us are committed to the gospel of Jesus, a gospel of peace and justice and love and brotherhood and sisterhood. The tough part is translating all that into action. Translating it into a community of faith which conducts worship and prayer and education and works of charity and social service. Translating it into a moral position on questions of public significance, impacting on the process by which legislation and public policy are made, because it is there that the basic work of justice is done in modern society. Both the pastoral task of building the Church and the political task of building the world involve choices, concrete and specific choices about how to spend our money, make our decisions, allocate our resources, direct our personal and collective allocation of time, treasure, and talent. None of us knows for sure how to do these things, none of us can be certain that our program of reform is exactly what the Lord intends for us today. So we have*

> *no choice, if we are to be a community of both faith and freedom, except to meet, debate, and make some decisions. That is what we are trying to do here. We are trying to begin a new way of doing the work of the Church in America.*[12]

The deep background for this moment can be found in the Americanist crisis of the 1890s, an important American chapter in the story of modern Catholicism "contending with modernity." Its outcome reinforced Catholicism's highly successful worldwide subcultural organizing strategy and cut short embryonic American efforts to explore the meaning of the democratic experience, especially the on-the-ground experience of religious freedom and social mobility. The pope ruled that there was not to be a Church in America different from the Church in the rest of the world, bishops would be more closely connected to the Vatican, and laypeople would remain outside the Church's governing structure and subordinate within its sacramental and pastoral practice. Bishops and priests were reminded that they were churchmen first of all, and formation and structure would reinforce a worldview and imagination that viewed the world and its history from the viewpoint of the Church. In the key Americanism encyclical of 1899, Pope Leo XIII specifically rejected proposals associated with Isaac Hecker to affirm the social and spiritual experience and ecclesial autonomy of laypeople. Convinced that the modern world was filled with enemies of the faith, the Church's European leaders consistently rejected proposals for sharing political responsibility, except where, as a minority group free from persecution, Catholics had little choice.[13]

There were many consequences of this episode, but I want to emphasize for our purposes today that it involved what we would today call a fundamental option for the Church. Of course, the impact of the encyclical was softened by excellent pastoral care, extraordinarily generous voluntary service of clergy and religious women, and ethnic mobilization creating rich subcultures to support family life and lay the groundwork for seizing opportunities for education and advancement when they became available. But Catholic religious meaning was located

---

12. Speech in *A Call to Action* (Washington, DC: USCC, 1976), 14.
13. The episode is summarized in James Hennessey, S.J., *American Catholics* (New York: Oxford University Press, 1980), and my assessment can be found in Isaac Hecker: *An American Catholic* (Mahwah, NJ: Paulist Press, 1992).

within the subculture of Church and those things intimately associated with the Church, sex, family, and charitable compassion for suffering. In one of the ironies of the much-lamented process of secularization, theology and pastoral practice combined to deprive lay experience, as lay, of religious meaning. That experience in the United States, seen in retrospect, included family histories of genuine transformation, from poverty and dependency to economic security and independence, from religious and cultural marginalization to full participation in American pluralism, from working-class struggles for justice to professional and institutional leadership and responsibility. Our families overcame poverty, gained access to the centers of power, and they kept the faith, they remained themselves. And make no mistake about it; today's American outsiders want very much to do the same.[14]

Contrary to a view widely held among American Catholic leaders, Catholic Americanization was not a failure, as if Catholics simply succumbed to the siren songs of materialism or lusted after acceptance by secular elites. No, the arrival of Catholic Americans was not about getting one of them to the White House and the rest to the Mall. It was a remarkable success story, indeed a story of liberation. And the large issue behind the Catholic version of the religion and politics question is how Catholics think about and imagine their historical trajectory.

The history of Catholic social and political thought and experience could be written around this question. John A. Ryan showed the American Church how to negotiate its dual Catholic and American loyalties, and John Courtney Murray and Bryan Hehir followed in his path. The brilliant liturgical reformer Virgil Michel worried about the dualism and hoped that liturgical reform could recover a sense of Catholic solidarity that would inspire Catholic commitment to serving God's whole human family in daily life. Down that road lay Archbishop Rembert Weakland's powerful reminder that the Church is the body of Christ, the very presence of God in America 24/7, when Catholics are workers and citizens and friends, not only when they are sheep with their shepherds. And the too-often forgotten Paul Hanley

14. This argument is being developed further in a series of papers delivered over the past several years, which will form the basis of a book on this subject. "The Missing Piece: The Renewal of Catholic Americanism," the 2006 Marianist Award Lecture at the University of Dayton, will be published by the university in 2008.

Furfey and his friend Dorothy Day puzzled over the way the Republican approach dulled the fangs of gospel radicalism. Down that road lay all those great-souled evangelical radicals who prevent shared civic responsibility from becoming simply wishy-washy, as it so often does. Nevertheless, Catholics remain disciples and citizens; most do not live in monasteries or Catholic Worker houses and wrestle with the dilemmas that have come with Americanization and professionalization and the responsibilities that accompany genuine freedom. Our post–World War II generation needed Pope John XXIII and Vatican II, and we needed Murray and Hehir and Dearden and Bernardin, who spoke as they did because they accompanied our families on their journeys from margin to mainstream. Now they and we together need to return to the big question posed at our moment in that journey: liberation for what? If we don't get the question right, I fear, we will find ourselves back in a subculture constructed around privatized religion and pseudoprophetic isolation.

One large question before us, then, is why 2004 developed as it did. Why was there not stronger support for "Faithful Citizenship"? Why have advocates of the Bernardin legacy made so little effort to influence the writing of the bishops' political responsibility statement for 2008? How has it come about that the Murray-Hehir-Bernardin position, once definitive of the American Catholic center, is now regarded as on the left of center, moving liberal Catholics like some of us here today to the left-wing edge of American Catholic political life?

These political questions constitute one aspect of the larger question of the current status and future prospects of American Catholicism. Let me offer a few suggestions and a few recommendations.

First, Jesuit sociologist John Coleman, in one of the finest essays on religion and politics written in the last generation, said that the Catholic Church lacked an adequate theology of citizenship.[15] Magisterial teachings on abortion, gay marriage, and embryonic stem cells are grounded in theology, and those teachings are clear on the demands of discipleship, too easily dismissive of the requirements of citizenship. The Vatican and the bishops have taken strong stands on war, poverty, economic justice, and more recently migration, but these issues are rarely spoken of in church and are clearly not considered definitive for

15. John A. Coleman, S.J., "The Catholic as Citizen," *Commonweal* (October 14, 1980).

Catholics. The pastoral letters of the 1980s and the string of political responsibility statements climaxing in "Faithful Citizenship" contained theologically grounded calls to nonviolence and an option for the poor, but they never found a theology that could affirm the lay life of lay Catholics. Instead, on abortion and related issues, the bishops offer countercultural claims asserted in a secular, and supposedly naked, public square. Once again it is evident, as it was to so many Christian Democrats in Europe and Latin America, that religious pluralism, political populism, and shared civic responsibility are not the default drives of the Catholic Church. Perhaps Coleman was right in arguing that Catholicism lacks an orthodox theology of citizenship.

Second, the lauded pastoral letters of the 1980s and the other texts fulfilled Murray's hope to help shape the public moral consensus, but they lacked a vigorous pastoral strategy. In commenting on those letters at the time, I took note of the growing use of countercultural language at odds with the ethic of shared responsibility informing the analytical sections. I argued that this countercultural imagination gave rise to strategies of exemption, not engagement. In the 1983 pastoral letter on nuclear weapons, for example, the final section offered warnings about the need to avoid the nuclear button but no ringing call to serious political participation. In the 1986 economics pastoral letter, positive language about lay Catholics finding holiness in bringing human dignity to life in the economy gave way in later drafts to a section on the family as a haven of anticonsumerist values in a materialistic America. This countercultural language set the stage for assertive claims on abortion and gay marriage, and on the left for nonviolence and the option for the poor, both of which made the respectful, nuanced, dualistic language of other texts seem indecisive, even wishy-washy.

Third, leaders of Catholic social ministry, even-handedly angry at Republican refusal of social responsibility and Democratic disrespect for pro-life advocates, have made a virtue of political homelessness. Voting against pro-choice politicians seems to some Catholics a requirement of Catholic political responsibility. In contrast, criticism of most available political options seems to accompany the consistent ethic of life, even among those actively lobbying legislatures on a wide range of domestic and foreign policy issues. To take one example of the consequences, no prominent Catholic institutional leaders came to the defense of Congressman David Obey, who had been a most helpful contact on many issues of interest to the hierarchy such as welfare reform, landmines, and debt forgiveness. Prominent bishops have without risk participated in a national prayer breakfast arranged by Republican Party officials, but young Catholics supporting "Faithful Citizenship" are publicly denounced as closet Democrats, scaring off potential supporters wary of appearing partisan.

Political homelessness for people of conscience may indeed be an unfortunate feature of contemporary political culture, but affirming that position may be one source of the widening culture of political disengagement and irresponsibility. Citizens and policymakers must make choices; homelessness is not a responsible option for those who love their country. One can try to change the parties or create a new one, but habitual moral criticism of politicians and politics, especially from religious leaders whose claims are grounded not just in faith but habits of peace and compassion, is a formula for democratic failure. Once again Coleman's point: do we have a theology that affirms the ambiguous choices built into democratic politics?

Fourth, while small cadres of politically conservative Catholics, some quite partisan, have worked effectively to influence Church policies and personnel, there has been a retreat from Church politics on the part of priests, religious, lay ministers, and formal and informal Church professionals. Many threw up their hands in despair during the 2004 election cycle, but only a few came to the support of younger activists seeking to support "Faithful Citizenship" much less to those organizing "Catholics for Kerry." In recent months, the bishops dramatically cut their support for the national episcopal conference; conservative Catholics savagely attacked the record of the late Congressman Robert Drinan, S.J.; and local hierarchies, nearly silent on the war and saying little of their own campaigns against poverty, spoke out forcefully against embryonic stem cell research and in favor of the traditional family—all with almost no protest from Catholic intellectuals and lay leaders. Only on immigration, where the Church's pastoral presence has produced an intelligent and at times courageous policy position, does there remain a hint of the constructive role the Church might yet play in American public life. On that issue, in Church politics, conservative influence has been offset by the growing and fairly well-organized Latino presence in the hierarchy, among a growing group of lay activists and some remarkable grass-roots organizations. Their effectiveness stands in stark contrast to the political paralysis of the vast majority of the Church professional and semiprofessional personnel.

Fifth, but perhaps most important in explaining the changing American Catholic political landscape, are changes in American-Vatican relations. In 1983 the Bernardin group was out front, and was at one point summoned to Rome to confer with the Vatican and brother NATO bishops. The hierarchy had always been nervously alert to Vatican anxieties, but ever so slowly leaders of our national episcopal conference began to engage in a two-way conversation with the Holy See. But the John Paul II era brought multiple directives on pastoral as well as doctrinal questions, apostolic visitations chilling to insecure bishops, and appointments of new bishops clearly related more to ecclesiastical politics than American pastoral imperatives. All this set the stage for political interventions, most notably one timed to influence "Faithful Citizenship," that defined the priority of the life issues and instructed bishops to call to account Catholic politicians when they consistently ignored Church teaching on nonnegotiable moral issues. When during the 2004 campaign the Communion issue divided the bishops, a committee chaired by Washington's Cardinal McCarrick looked to the Vatican for guidance. When McCarrick claimed Cardinal Ratzinger's support for local option, his claim was very publicly challenged, once again placing a chill on any who would venture too close to pro-choice politicians. As in Latin America, the Vatican has played an important role in changing the political orientation of the American hierarchy toward the assertion of distinctive Catholic claims and away from shared responsibility for the common good.

Conclusion

How one thinks about Catholic and politics depends in part on how one understands the trajectory of American Catholic history. As American Catholics after World War II moved up the socioeconomic ladder, out of the old urban neighborhoods and into the multiple centers of American society, their pastors regarded that movement with favor. Vatican II seemed to affirm a post-subcultural approach to mission and ministry that focused on engagement with issues of human dignity and global solidarity. As expected, Americanization eroded boundaries and weakened communal bonds, opening Catholics to American personalism, congregationalism, and interreligious fraternization. In 1971, I commended a pastoral strategy of "hanging loose" with what Andrew Greeley later called "do-it-yourself Catholics." Leading bishops and theologians hoped that a new sense of social and political responsibility, grounded in the experience of American arrival, would renew the American Church, a hope best expressed in Cardinal Dearden's bicentennial program. That vision has not worked out as expected, in part because an optimistic but challenging Americanist understanding of American Catholic history has given way to a more Catholic version of the story. In that version, Americanization was a process of adaptation to American culture fueled by an unworthy desire for acceptance and respectability, and the price was too high. Americanization was a process of secularization, with the loss of Catholic faith, the decline of Catholic practice, and the erosion of Catholic identity. Catholics, by this account, have loved America too much and their Church too little. The answer is to restate the boundaries between themselves and others, and re-imagine their distance from America's way of life.

Of course, Catholics must be themselves, but fulfillment of the promise of American Catholic life requires a more positive reading of family experiences of economic, social, and educational improvements, and far greater attention not only to America and Americans, but to the American part of our Church and ourselves. Certainly the Americanist idea is not just a simple celebration of Americanization. I often think that people like Dorothy Day and Daniel and Philip Berrigan, after a lifetime of attacks on national policies and symbols, were more American than their critics. The critics, at almost every fork in the road, choose to accept prevailing definitions of the possible. The radicals, loving America too much perhaps, really believed that their country's problems were their problems, its sins and graces their own. At a time when politics stumbles before the depth of national problems, we should be wary of analysis that ends up encouraging Catholic difference. Instead, we should recast the debate as one between those who care first for the integrity of the Church, and want to emphasize what makes Catholic different, and those who, as Catholics, care passionately about America and its romantic promise, care most about its people, Catholics among them. The question, then, is how we as a Catholic people regard the American people, and the American side of ourselves. That in the end is the sticking point of every Catholic's politics, always was, always will be.

4. The Common Good and the American Bishops' Guidelines

Kristin E. Heyer, Ph.D., Loyola Marymount University

> *Politics in this election year and beyond should be about an old idea with new power—the common good. The central question should not be, "Are you better off than you were four years ago?" It should be, "How can 'we'—all of us, especially the weak and vulnerable—be better off in the years ahead?"*[1]

Addressing American Catholics in "Faithful Citizenship," the U.S. bishops renew their call for a politics "focused on moral principles not on the latest polls, on the needs of the poor and vulnerable not the contributions of the rich and powerful, and on the pursuit of the common good not the demands of special interests."[2] My paper focuses on the meaning and significance of the principle of the common good, and its implications for political discernment for U.S. Catholics, in particular. I wish to suggest we consider the common good more in terms of a *lens* that can help refocus such discernment than as an end product that may appear too different to various groups to be meaningful. As the bishops suggest, pursuing the common good ushers in a new kind of politics, or rather, one reminiscent of an old kind of politics, such that the concept shapes our questions rather than predetermines our answers. This approach recalls a classical model of deliberative democracy that entails genuine engagement about what constitutes the good life, rather than the politics of self-interested bargaining or power plays a cynical public has come to expect. Shifting our focus via the common good can help move us from a model of "I want X" to "X would be good for the community to which we belong."[3]

As we shall see, using the principle of the common good as an interpretive lens helps attune us to features of our culture that challenge

1. U.S. Conference of Catholic Bishops, "Faithful Citizenship: A Catholic Call to Political Responsibility" (Washington, DC: USCCB), 2003, 2.
2. "Faithful Citizenship."
3. See Benjamin Barber, *Strong Democracy: Participatory Politics for a New Age* (Berkeley: University of California Press, 1984), 171.

fundamental Catholic values and to significant elements that too often get distorted or lost to view.[4] To that end my discussion will address three questions: (1) Why is the common good so important? (2) What does the Catholic tradition mean by the common good? and (3) What are the implications of a common good perspective for contemporary political issues such as economic and immigration policies?

Common Good Tradition: Its Significance

To begin with, why is the common good tradition so important for Catholics in particular? The social nature of the person, of human flourishing, and of salvation present key theological foundations for the significance of the Catholic common good tradition. This tradition is rooted in a vision of the human person as created in God's image, social and political by nature, and endowed with inviolable dignity and human rights. The bishops begin their discussion of Catholic social teaching in "Faithful Citizenship" with the fundamental principle of the dignity of human life: Every person is created in the image and likeness of God, so each person's life and dignity must be respected, whether that person worked in the World Trade Center or a market in Baghdad, or whether an unborn child or a convicted criminal on death row.[5]

According to this theological anthropology, humans are not only inherently sacred, but also fundamentally *social* by nature, born into a fabric of relationships and created to flourish in community. Catholic teaching acknowledges humans' radical interdependence. Biologically speaking, human children are among the most dependent creatures in all of creation. Beyond the confines of the family, we depend on our neighbors for things such as commerce, employment, mutual safety, friendship, and recreation. The significance of human interdependence is central to the principle of the common good and gets expressed in teachings on the most intimate sphere of family life outward to Catholic calls for institutional solidarity amid globalization.

This social emphasis is *theologically* grounded in the Christian belief in a Trinitarian God, for humans created in the image of that

---

4. See William A. Barbieri, Jr., "Beyond the Nations: The Expansion of the Common Good in Catholic Social Thought," *Review of Politics* 63, no. 4: 723–754; (Fall 2001): 750.
5. "Faithful Citizenship."

God are thus inherently social; to be a person is to be in relationship with other persons. Catholics also stress the mutual implication of mutuality and relationality: God is love; the degree to which humans actualize their capacity for love, mutual communion, solidarity, their goodness becomes more like God's.[6] Thus radical privacy becomes the ultimate enemy, and the marginalization of persons from participation in the life of community becomes the ultimate injustice. Michael Himes and Kenneth Himes describe the theological sacredness of the human person in words that well illustrate humanity's inherently social nature: "creation (our *common* origin), redemption (our *common* gift), discipleship (our *common* vocation), and eschatology (our *common* destiny)." As they note, "all these elements contribute to the communitarian vision of the Catholic tradition."[7]

In addition to a Trinitarian anthropology, in recent decades the Catholic tradition has increasingly emphasized the social dimension of human salvation.[8] The Second Vatican Council's Pastoral Constitution on the Church in the Modern World *(Gaudium et Spes)* emphasizes God's salvation of humans as members of a certain community, as a chosen people, "[since] God did not create [persons] for life in isolation, but for the formation of social unity."[9] Latin American liberation theologians have also highlighted the idea that "...people of faith do not stand before God alone, as individuals, but rather as members of a community of faith that has shared the truth that has shaped each member."[10] In a North American context we recall Martin Luther King's counsel: "[W]e go up together, or we go down together," and, "We, as a people, will get to the promised land." Thus our social nature is inherent, not extrinsic, for we find our fulfillment through participation in the shared life of a community. Because we are so thoroughly social, "no one of us flourishes unless all of us are flourishing."[11]

---

6. See David Hollenbach, S.J., *The Common Good and Christian Ethics* (New York: Cambridge University Press, 2002), 130–131.
7. Michael J. Himes and Kenneth R. Himes, O.F.M., *Fullness of Faith: The Public Significance of Theology* (New York: Paulist Press, 1993), 169 (emphasis added).
8. Todd David Whitmore, "Catholic Social Teaching: Starting With the Common Good," in Kathleen Maas Weigert and Alexia K. Kelley, *Living the Catholic Social Tradition* (Lanham, MD: Sheed & Ward, 2005), 59–86 at 60.
9. Second Vatican Council, *Gaudium et Spes*, 32.
10. Jon Sobrino, S.J., *The Principle of Mercy: Taking the Crucified Peoples from the Cross* (Maryknoll, NY: Orbis, 1994), 165–166.
11. Whitmore, 75.

In this context, human rights are not absolute claims made by radically autonomous individuals, but rather, claims to goods necessary for the person to participate with dignity in community life.[12] A Catholic articulation of human rights encompasses not only civil and political liberties, but also "thicker" social and economic rights, such as housing, health care, education, and employment. If the human person is not only sacred, but social, then how we organize our society—in economics, law, policy—directly affects human dignity and the capacity of individuals to grow in the fullness of human life. The common good flowing from this social theory is an expansive one, including shared goods that transcend the interests of individual nations, such as international peace, debt relief, and global commerce. Hence we have begun to move from the intrinsically social nature and destiny of the human person to the meaning of the common good that flows from these theological foundations.

The Meaning(s) of the Common Good

The principle of the common good is not a new or distinctively Catholic idea, of course. Classical Greek philosophy shaped a vision of "the good life," with Aristotle articulating the pursuit of the general welfare of the *polis,* or city-state, in a context of participatory self-governance, for example. Augustine and Aquinas built on this understanding but conceived of the ultimate good as the fullness of life in God, such that the earthly common good may be achieved only partially or analogously. Hence as the common good principle has evolved in Catholic thought, the order of the universal common good or spiritual *telos* of all persons remains distinct from, but related to, the order of the temporal, political common good. Therefore, Christians are called to be agents of the common good as friendships, family life, church, and a just society are all incomplete but anticipatory presences of the kingdom of God. For if salvation is a social phenomenon—"ultimate union with God and neighbor that images the communion between the persons of the Trinity"—then other more proximate forms of fulfillment in the here and now are social phenomena as well, "whether in the sphere of the family, economy, or shared political life."[13]

12. Himes and Himes, 46.
13. Whitmore, 62.

The Catholic social tradition has elaborated dimensions of the temporal common good in increasingly expansive ways over recent decades, incorporating a consideration of relations among sovereign states and questions of a global common good beginning in the 1960s. In his encyclical On Christianity and Social Progress *(Mater et Magistra)*, Pope John XXIII defines the common good as the sum total of those conditions of social living whereby men and women are enabled more fully and more readily to achieve their well-being.[14] At a fundamental level, the idea here is that "we can know a good in common that we cannot know alone."[15] I used to offer the example of clean air as something either we all enjoy or none of us enjoys, until I moved to Los Angeles where one's enjoyment of a smog-reduced environs directly depends on his or her proximity to breezy (and pricey) coastal locations. Yet prognoses about global warming or threats of infectious disease alert us to goods like a healthy environment that we may not privately enjoy—goods that we either enjoy together or squander together. From a central understanding that "[h]uman dignity can be realized and protected only in community,"[16] the common good principle suggests that some goods essential to human flourishing that transcend the arena of personal interaction, such as "political self-determination, genuine participation in economic productivity...enjoyment of one's cultural and linguistic heritage...cannot be directly obtained by individuals acting alone. Such goods accrue to individuals through their participation in the public life and institutions of society."[17] The Catholic tradition recognizes that political institutions hold significant responsibility for achieving the common good, connecting the very meaning of law and civil authority to the attainment of the common good.[18] Thus the

14. Pope John XXIII, On Christianity and Social Progress *(Mater et Magistra)*, 65.
15. Michael Sandel, *Liberalism and the Limits of Justice* (New York: Cambridge University Press, 1982), 183.
16. National Council of Catholic Bishops, "Economic Justice for All: A Pastoral Letter on Catholic Social Teaching and the U.S. Economy" (Washington, DC: United States Catholic Conference, 1986), no. 14.
17. John A. Coleman, S.J., "The Common Good and Catholic Social Thought," in Margaret O'Brien Steinfels, ed., *American Catholics & Civic Engagement: A Distinctive Voice* (Lanham, MD: Sheed & Ward, 2004), 3–18 at 12.
18. In On Establishing Universal Peace in Truth, Justice, Charity, and Liberty *(Pacem in Terris)*, Pope John XXIII states that "[t]he attainment of the common good is the sole reason for the existence of civil authorities" (54). Aquinas' very articulation law is as an ordinance of practical reason promulgated by legitimate authority for the common good (ST I-II, Q 90, art. 1, 23).

common good can be understood as an ensemble of conditions that enable human flourishing, including social and economic conditions that guarantee access to public goods and enable true social participation in all of the goods of society.[19]

It is critical to remember that pursuing the common good does *not* entail a simple utilitarian calculus of the greatest good for the greatest number. In contrast to the common good tradition, mere majoritarianism threatens to exclude individuals and groups, whereas participation of every member is central to Catholic common good theory. For this reason the common good is directly linked to the option for the poor and vulnerable, requiring not only that those on the periphery be included in society but also that their voices be heard.[20] The primary reason for this option for the poor in Catholic thought is not preference for preference's sake, but rather to incorporate disempowered and marginalized persons into full participation in the life of the community, "to enable *all* persons to share in and contribute to the common good."[21] Thus to those who attempt arguments in favor of outsourcing to *maquilas* in a global market, for example, asserting that "bad jobs are better than no jobs, poverty is better than misery, unclean air and polluted water are necessary byproducts of economic growth," the U.S. bishops have responded that "one failing does not justify another," for a common good framework calls us to do better in shaping a just development agenda.[22] For if "the dignity of persons can be realized only in community, genuine community, in its turn, can only exist where the substantial freedom and dignity of [every] human person is secured."[23]

As I mentioned at the outset, however, the common good refers not only to outcomes like the *telos* of a given community or policies enabling fulfillment, but it also serves as a *lens* that helps us to perceive and discern. It is particularly important to consider the common good

---

19. John A. Coleman, S.J., "The Future of Catholic Social Thought" in Kenneth R. Himes, O.F.M., ed., *Modern Catholic Social Teaching: Commentaries and Interpretations* (Washington, DC: Georgetown University Press, 2005), 522–544 at 538.
20. Whitmore, 72.
21. See NCCB, "Economic Justice for All," no. 88.
22. Cardinal Theodore McCarrick, "Labor Day 2004: Global Trade That Works for All" (September 6, 2004), http://www.catholiclabor.org/laborday/laborday-04.htm (accessed May 24, 2007).
23. Coleman, "The Common Good and Catholic Social Thought," 13.

as a criterion[24] or a process when we consider its relevance to political discernment in a context marked by the dominant influence of individualism (the American way) and self-interest (the human condition). What does it mean to consider the common good as a hermeneutical lens or as a process? If the common good refers to conditions and institutions that enable human flourishing, it must also entail interactive conversation about the goods we pursue in common.[25] In Drew Christiansen's words, the common good principle "does not offer an already-out-there, ready-to-be-grasped norm of justice but rather a set of goals to be arrived at through open debate and public consensus."[26] Such deliberate engagement constitutes both a route toward and a characteristic of a good community, that is, a place where people genuinely depend on one another through decision-making about their common purposes.[27] Vatican II affirmed the deep roots of a vision of good life in the gospel, and it also upheld the possibility of bringing Christian convictions about the common good into fruitful engagement with alternate conceptions, calling for dialogue with the sciences, diverse cultures, and other religions.[28]

Yet, are such processes and frameworks destined to remain incommensurably "red" or "blue," depending on which side of the state line or political party we inhabit? In other words, does not the pluralism that characterizes our nation, much less world, render a concept like the common good hopelessly idealistic at best? Because the common good does not refer to a static outcome but encompasses these meanings of process and lens with an increasingly expansive scope, "the quest for a common good takes place *within* and not *against* the ex-

24. In "Beyond the Nations," Barbieri similarly describes the common good as referring both "...to the *telos* of a given community—that goal or end-state toward which it aspires" as well as to "a *criterion* for evaluating various courses of action in the here and now" (728).
25. Dennis McCann, "The Good to Be Pursued in Common," in Oliver F. Williams and John W. Houck, eds., *The Common Good and U.S. Capitalism* (Lanham, MD: University Press of America, 1987), 158–178.
26. Drew Christiansen, S.J., "The Common Good and the Politics of Self-Interest: A Catholic Contribution to the Practice of Citizenship," in Donald L. Gelpi, S.J., *Beyond Individualism: Toward a Retrieval of Moral Discourse in America* (Notre Dame, IN: University of Notre Dame Press, 1989), 54–86 at 82.
27. Hollenbach, *The Common Good and Christian Ethics,* 42.
28. For a helpful discussion of the impact of Vatican II on this particular conception of the common good (which he terms "dialogic universalism"), see Hollenbach, *The Common Good and Christian Ethics*, chapter 6.

perience of plurality."[29] Pluralism is, in fact, essential to the common good "because different communities center on the pursuit of different components of the complex human good; because institutional diversity facilitates extensive participation in social life; and because no one association can claim to be a perfect community."[30] In John Courtney Murray's discussion of the common good in his text, *We Hold These Truths*, for which this conference is named, he uses the metaphor of conversation. He urges civil conversation about the truths we hold in common across our different "life worlds."[31] Confronted with an atmosphere of religious pluralism whose intellectual experience was confusion, Murray sought not to eliminate pluralism, but, as he put it, to clarify real pluralisms so that we would not have "ignorant armies clashing by night," but persons locked together in genuine argument, a truly *civil* society. More recently, David Hollenbach has termed this common pursuit of a shared vision of the good life *intellectual solidarity.* Use of the concept of the common good today in an effort to similarly clarify competing values and seriously engage fundamental questions would help move beyond the strategic rhetoric and reductionistic sound bites that characterize contemporary political discourse. Moreover, a Catholic practice of intellectual solidarity should be characterized by virtues of hospitality and humility rather than suspicion or coercion.

Before moving to applications, I want to briefly highlight several challenges to a common good approach particular to our own context, for Catholic communitarian values encounter a difficult reception in a setting that prizes individual liberty. While the Catholic vision shares certain commitments of a democracy like the United States, it radically challenges a culture that prioritizes economic efficiency over solidarity with the weak and marginalized, or narrow national interest over global concern. Americans' tendency to favor moral privatism and individualistic theories of material success and failure reflects a libertarian worldview that departs significantly from an outlook informed by the common good.

---

29. Philip Selznick, *The Moral Commonwealth* (Berkeley: University of California Press, 1992), 538.
30. Brian Stiltner, *Religion and the Common Good* (Lanham, MD: Rowman & Littlefield, 1999), 178.
31. See John Courtney Murray, S.J., *We Hold These Truths: Catholic Reflections on the American Proposition* (New York: Sheed & Ward, 1960), esp. 103–139.

Our culture of individualism, influenced by classical liberalism, is premised on the idea that unencumbered, autonomous individuals form "contracts" to associate with one another as it serves each one's best interest or out of a need for self-preservation amid a Hobbesian war of all against all. Even Lockean rights to "life, liberty and property" remain *individual* rights, and persons come together to protect such rights out of self-interest.[32] The all-American credo that we pull up our bootstraps and make our own fate is perhaps as entrenched as it is incompatible with a solidaristic idea that we share each other's fate. A penchant for explaining poverty by individual behaviors such as laziness or irrational choices alone, for example, challenges structural analyses and restricts moral matters to individual virtue and vice. As Hollenbach highlights in his book on the common good, recent social scientific research that indicates two-thirds of Americans consider morality a private matter refutes the belief that the good of the individual is inseparable from the good of his or her community. This tendency leads Hollenbach to lament that, for most Americans, "there is little reason to be concerned about the quality of public life," much less understand the good life as something commonly pursued or shared.[33] An emphasis on private virtue "minimize[s] the moral substance of our public world, the way our institutions empower or impoverish, emancipate or debase."[34]

A libertarian worldview elevates personal freedom as the highest value a society should seek. The Catholic tradition does not deny the importance of human freedom or individual rights, but because humans are inherently social, human rights are primarily realized in community and rights are matched by corresponding duties to contribute to the common good. Thus there also exists a far more robust connection between the role of the government and the common good than a libertarian notion of the government as an unwelcome intruder, or the American attitude that the government that governs least governs best. The disdain for Washington professed even by political candidates is matched by a "live-and-let-live" ethos that prizes

32. Whitmore, 61. See Thomas Hobbes, *Leviathan*, ed. C. B. MacPherson (Harmondsworth, England: Penguin, 1986), 185 and 189; and John Locke, *Second Treatise of Government*, ed. Peter Laslett (Cambridge, UK: Cambridge University Press, 1960), sections 128–130.
33. Hollenbach, *The Common Good and Christian Ethics*, 27.
34. Franklin I. Gamwell, "Calling for the Common Good," *Living Pulpit* 5:2 (April–June 1996): 22–23 at 22.

tolerance as its highest virtue and privacy as its first right. A culture in which "good fences make good neighbors" significantly hinders deliberative engagement about shared goods, in local much less global terms. Such a libertarian ethos (combined with isolationism, a free market culture, and the relative apathy of "the have's") not only contradicts the social foundation of the Catholic tradition as previously outlined, but it also remains insufficient for addressing the trenchant problems we face as a nation and world. In light of these cultural challenges to a communitarian ethos, the value of a common good framework that supplies a corrective bias in evaluating prospective courses of action becomes even more apparent.[35]

Implications of the Common Good: Economic Policy

To begin again with the bishops' own words from "Faithful Citizenship":

> *In a world where one-fifth of the population survives on less than one dollar per day...and where poverty, corruption, and repressive regimes bring untold suffering to millions of people, we simply cannot remain indifferent. As a wealthy and powerful nation, the United States has the capacity and the responsibility to address this scandal of* ***poverty and underdevelopment.*** *As a principal force in globalization, we have a responsibility to* ***humanize globalization,*** *and to spread its benefits to all, especially the world's poorest, while addressing its negative consequences.*[36]

In their recent document "A Place at the Table," the bishops make concrete the dizzying statistics that detail a widening gap between rich and poor:

> *Poverty is not just about numbers. It is about parents who cannot feed their children in Latin America or who are unable to bring sick or disabled children to a doctor in the United States. It is about the devastating consequences of addiction and family violence, about AIDS orphans in Africa, and about "no-parent*

35. Barbieri, "Beyond the Nations," 749–50.
36. "Faithful Citizenship," 26.

> *families" in the United States. This is not about having a new car or about how fast you can get on the Internet; rather, this is about having a decent place to live, enough to eat, clean water in your village, and clean air in your community.*[37]

Examining economic policy issues through the lens of the common good tradition leads us to employ rather different criteria than reigning paradigms that maximize profit or even insist on strict impartiality. Let us turn to a few brief examples from local to global levels.

Pursuing the common good requires American Catholics to understand that economic and social rights flow from the affirmation of universal human dignity and sociality—rights to a job with decent conditions and pay, to health care, to education. It also means the rights articulated in Catholic thought frequently correspond to duties that set limits on individual rights. For example, because of beliefs about the universal destination of created goods, the economic right to private property is real but not absolute; there is said to be a "social mortgage" on the goods of creation. Thus, for example, Todd Whitmore has elaborated a "maximum living wage" in light of Catholic social teaching, setting limits not on how much income one earns, but rather on how much of that wealth one uses for one's own living, insisting that the rest belongs to the common good, such that the good to oneself and one's family is not disproportionate to or out of harmony with that larger good.[38]

Catholic teaching does not require absolute equality of outcomes for every member of society, but the tradition's shift to relative egalitarianism does mean that there are moral limits on the range of inequalities that exist and differences permitted.[39] This shift presupposes that "equality best facilitates harmony and therefore...it is inequality that must be explained."[40] Hence minimum and maximum thresholds help enhance the unity and solidarity of human communities and diminish divisiveness.[41] In writings from Pope John XXIII to Pope John Paul II,

---

37. USCCB, "A Place at the Table: A Catholic Recommitment to Overcome Poverty and to Respect the Dignity of All God's Children" (November 13, 2002) (Washington, DC: USCCB, 2002), 4–5.
38. Whitmore, 75.
39. See Drew Christiansen, "On Relative Equality: Catholic Egalitarianism after Vatican II," *Theological Studies,* 45 (1984): 651–75 at 653.
40. Whitmore, 67. See also Christiansen, "On Relative Equality."
41. Himes and Himes, 175.

we witness a shift away from a presumption of hierarchy and encounter a focus on the gap between the rich and the poor or the powerful and weak as a matter of particular concern in all spheres of society.[42] According to such teaching, inequality facilitates injustice to the extent it denies groups or individuals the ability to fully participate in the life of civil society's institutions, a key component of the common good.[43]

Wage differentials provide a concrete illustration of the limits a common good perspective should impose. In 1960, CEO salaries in this country averaged twelve times those of employees in production-level, nonsupervisory positions. In 1980, that pay gap had increased to a ratio of 45:1, and in 2004, 300:1.[44] With the recent passage of the first minimum wage increase in more than a decade, the United States will finally (gradually) end the second-longest period in our nation's history during which the minimum wage has not increased. The federal minimum wage has remained $5.15 per hour since 1997. Thus alongside skyrocketing productivity during the last decade we have witnessed a decline in the real value of wages, leaving 37 million living in poverty in the United States, with 45 million without health insurance. In 2004, the minimum wage amounted to 33 percent of the average hourly wage of American workers, its lowest level since 1949.[45]

Catholic support for a living wage, which Pope John Paul II called the critical criterion for determining the legitimacy of the entire economic system,[46] reflects fundamental values of human dignity and the dignity of work, along with the belief that work should be an *escape* from poverty, not another version of it.[47] The tradition insists that while wages are only one component of the overall business paradigm, and businesses need profits to stay afloat, the maximization of profit by way of squeezing workers is unjust.[48] Again, the Catholic tradition does not demand flat equality, but a commitment to the common good

42. Whitmore, 69.
43. In "Economic Justice for All," the bishops frame social justice in precisely such terms, noting "Basic justice demands establishment of minimum levels of participation in the life of the human community for all persons" (no. 77).
44. John P. Hogan, *Credible Signs of Christ Alive: Case Studies from the Catholic Campaign for Human Development* (Lanham, MD: Sheed & Ward, 2002), 41.
45. Economic Policy Institute Issue Guide, July 2004, http://www.epinet.org/content.cfm/issueguides_minwage_minwagefaq (accessed June 5, 2007).
46. Pope John Paul II, On Human Work *(Laborem Exercens)*, 1981.
47. USCCB, "A Place at the Table."
48. Hogan, 41.

does contest such growing disparities, calling instead for the employer-employee relationship to be marked by mutual respect and dignity. As one example, in contrast to the CEO of a major American retailer whose 2005 reported salary was 871 times as high as the corporation's domestic workers and 50,000 times as high as its Chinese workers, Costco's CEO has pledged to earn no more than 12 times the typical person working on the floor. This reflects an admirable commitment to the values embraced by a common good perspective.

In light of his community-organizing work for a living wage with low-income residents in northern Virginia, Rabbi Jack Moline invokes the Jewish prophets: "Countless times in the Torah we are reminded not to mistreat the worker, not to exploit the laborer, not to oppress the poor.... Servitude does not mean working without compensation. It means working without adequate compensation, without the wherewithal to provide for the needs of one's self and one's family."[49] Working several jobs at the stagnant minimum wage only to remain in poverty does not foster the authentic human development central to the common good.

A Christian understanding of stewardship and the common good thus has implications for our decisions in the workplace and voting booth alike. Our Catholic lens demands we understand the federal budget as a moral document and that we evaluate tax policies based on how equitably they distribute the burden for sustaining institutions and programs to meet human need. Again an outlook shaped by the common good also attunes us to distorting ideologies. For example, Pope John Paul II frequently warned about the dangers of greed, a preoccupation with "having rather than being," and an addiction to things that desensitizes us to the plight of others around the planet.

Furthermore, if "we really are all responsible for all," a Catholic commitment to a *global* common good has economic implications as well. At the international level, we witness perhaps even starker challenges to a presumption of relative equality. Therefore, American voters are called to judge policies by how well they enable sustainable development and counter existing patterns of degradation and marginalization. For instance, Vatican officials and the U.S. bishops alike have critiqued free trade policies that focus only on market forces and

49. Ibid., 34.

aggravate global inequalities with practices such as harmful agricultural subsidies for rich countries' own farmers. A common good perspective bids Catholics to support just trade policies that prioritize the sustainable growth of the economies of developing countries.[50]

The Church's jubilee campaign for debt relief served as a concrete countersign to the contemporary reality for so many developing nations enslaved in debt; recent estimates indicate that for every $1 sent to poor countries in aid, $1.30 flows back to the United States in lender debt interest, a type of reverse foreign aid. Finally, concern for the common good challenges all forms of globalization that reinforce inequality and existing patterns of exclusion. Joseph Nye has called the limitation of membership in the International Monetary Fund and World Trade Organization to political and economic elites "globalization's democratic deficit."[51] If the primary Catholic meaning of justice is participation, we must develop institutions that will enable marginalized persons to have a greater voice in shaping policies and institutions that directly affect them.

Implications of the Common Good: Immigration Policy

Global underdevelopment and the impact of international trade policies directly relate to another pressing political issue with economic and moral dimensions: immigration. A common good perspective does not provide a facile solution to pending negotiations over how to handle the estimated 12 million undocumented immigrants presently residing in the United States, nor a predetermined calculus for balancing the needs of the national common good against our duties to a more universal common good. Catholic teaching does, however, set clear limits on legitimate reasons for exclusion and calls us to hospitality and justice rooted in its biblical and encyclical traditions.

Very briefly, the formative liberation of Israel by God from enslavement by the Egyptians led to commandments regarding hospitality to strangers (see Exodus 23:9; Leviticus 19:33). When Joseph, Mary, and

50. Statement by Archbishop Celestino Migliore on October 17, 2006, to the meeting of the U.N. General Assembly on international trade and development. Full text of statement available at http://www.holyseemission.org/17Oct2006.html (accessed November 17, 2006).
51. Hollenbach, "The Life of the Human Community," *America* (November 4, 2002): 6–8 at 8.

Jesus flee to Egypt, the émigré Holy Family becomes the archetype for every refugee family.[52] In Jesus' parables, such as the Good Samaritan and the Last Judgment, he identifies neighbor love and just living with care for the vulnerable stranger among us. In his recent encyclical On Christian Love *(Deus Caritas Est)*, Pope Benedict XVI reminds us that neighbor love enjoined by the Good Samaritan parable can no longer be limited to "the closely knit community of a single country or people." Rather, "Anyone who needs me, and whom I can help, is my neighbor....Love of God and love of neighbor have become one: In the least of the brethren we find Jesus himself, and in Jesus we find God."[53] Thus who constitutes our neighbor(s) does not depend on birthplace or possession of documents.[54]

Grounded in this scriptural heritage and in its expansive understanding of human rights and the common good as the end of the political community, the Catholic social tradition upholds twin rights to emigration and immigration, placing the onus on states that would restrict immigration to make the moral case for exclusion. Included in the tradition's articulation of social and economic rights is the affirmation that persons have the right to fulfill those rights in their homeland; if they cannot support themselves or their families in their country of origin, they possess the right to migrate to do so.[55] This right to migrate is also rooted in the universal destination of created goods, such that state sovereignty "cannot be exaggerated" to the point that access to land is denied to needy people from other nations, provided that the national common good "rightly understood" does not forbid it.[56] A key component of the right to migrate, then, is its

---

52. Pope Pius XII, On the Spiritual Care to Migrants *(Exsul Familia Nazarethana)* (September 30, 1952), in *The Church's Magna Charta for Migrants,* ed. Rev. Giulivo Tessarolo, PSSC (Staten Island, NY: St. Charles Seminary, 1962), introduction.

53. Pope Benedict XVI, On Christian Love *(Deus Caritas Est)* (December 25, 2005), 15; http://www.vatican.va/holy_father/benedict_xvi/encyclicals/documents/hf_ben-xvi_enc_20051225_deus-caritas-est_en.html.

54. Bishop Nicholas DiMarzio, Chair, U.S. Bishops' Committee on Domestic Policy, "Labor Day Statement 2006" in *Origins* 36, no. 13 (September 7, 2006): 201–204 at 204.

55. See Pope John XXIII, On Establishing Universal Peace in Truth, Justice, Charity, and Liberty *(Pacem in Terris;* April 11, 1963), 106. All encyclical citations are taken from David J. O'Brien and Thomas A. Shannon, *Catholic Social Thought: The Documentary Heritage* (Maryknoll, NY: Orbis), 1992, unless otherwise indicated. See also "Strangers No Longer," no. 34–35.

56. Pope Pius XII, On the Spiritual Care to Migrants *(Exsul Familia Nazarethana)*, 51, citing 1948 Vatican Letter to U.S. Bishops and *Pacem in Terris.*

inclusion of economic rights violations alongside political oppression as legitimate causal factors.[57]

While the social tradition of the Catholic Church recognizes the right of sovereign nations to control their borders, as with the right to private property, this is not an absolute right. In their recent pastoral letter "Strangers No Longer: Together on the Journey of Hope," the U.S. and Mexican bishops' conferences emphasize the presumption of migration and reception over sovereignty in light of the contemporary situation of global poverty and persecution.[58] They judge nations like the United States, "which have the ability to protect and feed their residents [to] have a stronger obligation to accommodate migration flows."[59] The bishops' conferences assert that the right of a sovereign state to control its borders to promote the common good and the human right to migrate in order to realize God-given rights are complementary, for while reasonable limits may be set, the common good is served when basic human rights are not violated.

Certainly there exists a level of complexity with respect to how exactly the Church's defense of "borderless" rights should be implemented in our contemporary situation, yet a commitment to universal human rights prohibits prioritizing the national to the international common good for the sake of greed rather than need. Narrow nationalism may not justify exclusion in the face of dire poverty. Many have noted that a North American focus on deterrence has not only proven ineffective, but it has also failed to "...alleviate the political, economic, and social factors that encourage or necessitate international migration."[60] At

57. The 1969 Instruction on Pastoral Care asserts that "where a state which suffers from poverty combined with great population cannot supply such use of goods to its inhabitants...people possess a right to emigrate, to select a new home in foreign lands and to seek conditions of life worthy of man [sic]." Sacred Congregation for Bishops, *Instruction on Pastoral Care*, no. 14. For a helpful discussion of Catholic teaching on economic refugees, see Drew Christiansen, S.J., "Sacrament of Unity: Ethical Issues in the Pastoral Care of Migrants and Refugees," in Office of Pastoral Care of Migrants and Refugees, Bishops' Committee on Migration, National Conference of Catholic Bishops, *Today's Immigrants and Refugees: A Christian Understanding* (Washington, DC: United States Catholic Conference, 1988), 81–114 at 90–91.

58. USCCB and *Conferencia del Episcopado Mexicano*, "Strangers No Longer: Together on the Journey of Hope: A Pastoral Letter Concerning Migration from the Catholic Bishops of Mexico and the United States," (2003), no. 39.

59.. Ibid., no. 36.

60. Maura Ryan, "Boundaries or Barriers? U.S. Immigration Policy and the Challenge of Solidarity" in Ryan and Todd David Whitmore, eds., *The Challenge of Global Stewardship: Roman Catholic Responses* (South Bend, IN: University of Notre Dame Press, 1997), 210–233 at 213.

present, the U.S. bishops and their allies in the "Justice for Immigrants Campaign" have called for comprehensive reform of current immigration laws and policies to better respond to "the realities of separated families and labor demands that compel people to immigrate to the United States, whether in an authorized or unauthorized fashion." They support the following initiatives: (1) an earned legalization program, (2) a new worker visa program that protects labor rights, (3) reform of the family-based preference system to ensure timely reunification, (4) restoration of due process protections for immigrants, and (5) policies that address the root causes of migration.[61]

Hence in 2007 the U.S. bishops and other Catholic groups lobbied in support of amendments to the Comprehensive Immigration Reform Act of 2007 (S. 1348) that strengthen family unity and ensure due process rights for immigrants impacted by enforcement raids, and in opposition to amendments that limit the number of persons eligible for the "Z visa" legalization program. Continuing to prevent immigrant workers from attaining or maintaining family unity treats them as mere economic units, rather than recognizing their full humanity. Sustained family separation does not serve the common good, as it has a negative impact on the social fabric within the United States as well as in the home countries of immigrants.

Using our lens attunes us both to the concrete demands of the universal common good and focuses on prevalent distortions that impact immigration policy. As the U.S. and Mexican bishops note, "Part of the process of conversion of mind and heart deals with confronting attitudes of cultural superiority, indifference, and racism; accepting migrants not as foreboding aliens, terrorists, or economic threats, but rather as persons with dignity and rights, revealing the presence of Christ; and recognizing migrants as bearers of deep cultural values and rich faith traditions."[62] To place social sins such as xenophobia "in the context of the common good, then, means not simply to view them as behavioral failures that require exhorting individuals...to mutual friendship, benevolence, and aid, but rather as parts of an overall puzzle involving social structures and collective action."[63] Hence rather than

---

61. USCCB, *Justice for Immigrants: A Journey of Hope* campaign "Justice for Immigrants," http://www.justiceforimmigrants.org/faq_cath_position.html (accessed May 29, 2007).
62. USCCB, "Strangers No Longer," no. 40.
63. Barbieri, 749.

simply perceiving the "problem" as illegal immigrants sapping public resources or threatening security, and the solution as greater fortification of the border or harsher punitive measures, genuine intellectual solidarity converts our perspective to identifying as true problems the dire poverty driving migrants to leave home to secure their families' survival and the wide-scale exploitation of day laborers within our borders. This conversion also shifts our focus away from criminalization and fortification and toward identifying lasting structural solutions such as global development, trade marked by justice, worker protections, and paths to citizenship for those already here.

The option a common good perspective makes on behalf of the vulnerable turns our attention toward enabling the participation of the marginalized regardless of legal status, particularly those who survive harrowing border crossings only to experience exploitation in our legal system and labor market (including individuals' rights *not* to migrate). The transcendent *telos* of the common good helps us to refrain from enshrining current law as eternal or elevating it to an idolatrous status. A framework rooted in a biblical justice that is relational, effusive, and marked by mercy prompts us to challenge the near-universal framing of amnesty as a contemptible procedure, and to move beyond pitting the rights of U.S. workers against those of international workers.

Conclusion

Multifaceted in strategy, a Catholic ethic is eminently holistic; the common good tradition sheds light on the interrelated nature not only of issues such as globalization and migration, as above, but also the relationship of poverty to varieties of violence, of patterns of consumption to environmental degradation, and so forth. A lived commitment to the implications of our common origin and destiny will bring the common good as process to the center of our joint deliberation about shared goods and the conditions that might realize them.

Political discernment in light of the common good can help Catholics to envision structures that enable all to flourish, especially those on the margins. As we have observed, using a lens of the common good expands our perspective to a global one that makes demands on us in the cause of justice as participation. It also brings into sharper focus distorting ideologies that can blur our vision. Finally, it helps us to perceive more acutely where we are going and where we want to go, together.

5. Working for Peace

Reverend Kenneth R. Himes, O.F.M, Ph.D., Boston College

In their statement, *Faithful Citizenship*, the U.S. Conference of Catholic Bishops address a number of concerns that ought to be issues for conscientious Catholic citizens in an election year. Under the heading "Moral Priorities for Public Life," they state the following:

> *Catholic teaching calls on us to work to* ***avoid war.*** *Nations must protect the right to life by finding ever more effective ways to prevent conflicts from arising, to resolve them by peaceful means, and to promote post-conflict reconstruction and reconciliation. All nations have a right and duty to defend human life and the common good against terrorism, aggression, and similar threats.... While military force as a last resort can sometimes be justified to defend against aggression and similar threats to the common good, we have raised serious moral concerns and questions about* ***preemptive or preventive use of force.***[1]

Catholic teaching is a complex mix of measured and limited support for military force, alongside growing emphasis on the value of nonviolence and expanding interest in what is commonly called *peacebuilding*. It is not a moral tradition that can be easily summarized, and it is certainly not a tradition that permits reduction to a TV sound bite or a bumper sticker slogan.

In this reflection I will address the topic of working for peace under three main headings: the meaning of peace, the contemporary developments within Catholic social teaching on peace, and the emergence of peacebuilding as a new theme. I will conclude with some questions concerning the ethics of war and peace that Catholics in the United States must reflect on if we are to practice faithful citizenship.

The Meaning of Peace

One difficulty we can encounter as Catholics within the wider political discourse is that our understanding of words is not always the same as

1. U.S. Conference of Catholic Bishops, "Faithful Citizenship: A Catholic Call to Political Responsibility" (Washington, DC: USCCB, 2003), 18–19.

the popular usage. A good example of that is *peace.* For most Americans, *peace* is what you have when the shooting stops. *Peace* is what exists when you do not have war. That understanding is not what the Catholic tradition means by *peace.*

Within Catholic thinking the word *peace* is best understood not in a negative way—as the absence of war—but in a positive sense, as the creation and promotion of a particular vision of peace. This positive sense draws on the writings of both Scripture and the patristic era.

In Hebrew the word for peace is *shalom,* and this term encompasses far more than the absence of violence. *Shalom* refers to a community experiencing a full and rich life. Shalom is a state of abundance wherein all the members of the community are able to enter into a shared life that is materially adequate, spiritually rich, and relationally satisfying. When people live together in fidelity to the covenant between God and God's people, and they know the blessings of God's generosity, then they are said to live in peace *(shalom).*

New Testament writings present peace as a dimension of the reign of God. Peace is God's gift to us through the ministry of Jesus, who regularly wishes peace as a greeting to his disciples and urges them to use it in the same way as they go forth into the world (see Luke 10:1–9). Peace is a gracious outcome when the followers of Jesus live in accord with the norms of the reign of God.

So for the biblical authors, the experience of peace entails far more than putting down one's weapons; it requires building up a community that offers its members a richly rewarding taste of divine blessing and human well-being.

Early church writers, such as Saint Augustine, carry forward the positive sense of peace. He uses the Latin word *pax* or peace in one or another form more than 2,500 times in his writings.[2] Several aspects of Augustine's understanding of peace merit notice.

First, peace is multidimensional. There is the peace that can be called eschatological, related to the final end of humankind in enjoyment of life with God. This eternal peace is beyond the reach of temporal life and human achievement. The peace that is available to humanity in this life also has its origin and destiny in God. It has, however, been corrupted due to sin and as such retains a weakened

2. Donald X. Burt, O.S.A., "Peace," in *Augustine Through the Ages: An Encyclopedia,* ed. Allan Fitzgerald, O.S.A. (Grand Rapids, MI: Eerdmans, 1999), 629.

connection to the first kind of peace. Yet it is real and it is a blessing when attained in earthly existence.

This earthly peace, discussed in Book XIX of *The City of God*, is what Augustine calls "civil peace."[3] It is a particular incarnation of the form of all peace, namely, *tranquillitas ordinis*. The tranquillity of order is attained when there is a proper ordering of each part in relation to the whole. Thus, there is a peace of the individual, of the family, of the city, and of the world. When one achieves civil peace the citizens of the political community are in right relation with each other, as well as with the subunits that make up the community and the higher units of which the community is a part. There is a right order existing among family, city, state and, ultimately, God.

For Augustine, the goal of any war is peace. He does not mean eschatological peace, but the peace of political communities living in history. The peace of the eschaton entails spiritual peace that is beyond the attainment of the earthly city. The aim of the earthly city is temporal peace, a civil peace that includes material and historical goods such as food, shelter, safety, and nonviolence. The goal of civil peace is to permit human community to develop and flourish.

In the biblical and Augustinian texts, we can see certain aspects of the Catholic view of peace that continue in their development of the tradition right to the present time:

- Peace is understood as a positive reality, entailing the establishment of justice and right order in and between societies.
- Peace is a universal human desire and is more fundamental than either war or violence. Humans are capable of peace and war is not inevitable, even if conflict is.
- There can be a false peace. The mere absence of violence is not peace since there may still be serious injustice in a society and an oppressive fear that prevents violence but that cannot be equated with genuine peace.
- Because peace is not simply the absence of violence it is not self-contradictory to speak of fighting for peace. Peace may require the use of violent force in order to establish justice and resist aggression.

---

3. Augustine, *The City of God* (New York: Modern Library Classics, 2000), Book XIX, ch. 13.

- War cannot create peace. At best, war can be used as a means of removing obstacles to peace, but war cannot of itself create the tranquillity of order that is true peace.

Contemporary Catholic Teaching on Peace

Church teaching regarding peace and war has evolved through several stages. In the earliest era of Christianity there was a profound resistance to approving violence and war as acceptable. By the time of Augustine there was an acknowledgment on the part of many believers that war might be acceptable under limiting conditions. The writings of Augustine and other patristic authors addressed what those conditions might be. This was the onset of Christian reflection within what has been called the "just war tradition."

Essentially, the just war tradition is a set of theories, differing in some details, that all make an argument that war can be morally justifiable. The various theories may answer differently the questions when, why, and how war may be acceptable. These theories share the foundational conviction that under some conditions war is morally acceptable. The just war tradition became the dominant mode of thinking used by the Church from the fourth century onward.

In the twentieth century, the experience of modern war and its resultant devastation presented a challenge to just war thinking. Could an ethical tradition originating in an age before modern weaponry and militaristic nation-states still be an apt guide for moral reflection? Amid that discussion the Catholic bishops of the world meeting at the Second Vatican Council called for "an evaluation of war with an entirely new attitude."[4] This new attitude did not necessarily mean opposing all war. The bishops at the Council also stated that, "As long as the danger of war remains and there is no competent and sufficiently powerful authority at the international level, governments cannot be denied the right to legitimate defense," presuming that peaceful measures to avoid war have been tried.[5]

What the new attitude can be understood to mean is the establishment of a presumption against war. Starting with John XXIII and continuing through the papacies of Paul VI, John Paul II, and

4. Second Vatican Council, Pastoral Constitution on the Church in the Modern World (*Gaudium et Spes*), 80.
5. Ibid., 79.

now Benedict XVI a teaching developed "that a presumption against war lies at the very center of Catholic thinking on war and peace."[6] Whereas some earlier theories of just war gave the presumption to justice, and war was understood as being morally neutral as a means to establish justice, the present formulation of the Church's teaching with the presumption against war reflects the "new attitude" called for at Vatican II. In short, seeing the idea of a just war within the context of modern war's destructive power has led the Catholic Church to voice much stronger opposition to resorting to war, in addition to affirming a greater commitment to developing alternative ways of securing a true peace.

Another important development in the Church's teaching that occurred at Vatican II was the acceptance of pacifism as a legitimate option for Christian conscience. Accepting the sincerity of those who find any approval of war difficult, the bishops gave their support to a conscientious rejection of all war on the part of individual believers. Adherents to pacifism, like those to just war theory, are bound to seek a genuine and true peace. The refusal to take up arms cannot be justified on the basis of indifference to a just peace, but only on the basis of a firm conviction that methods other than war are the appropriate means to a true peace. The positive nature of peace continues to be affirmed as the proper end of those seeking the good of human flourishing; the disagreement lies at the level of seeing war as a possible means to the end.

Yet another significant development in the contemporary treatment of peace in Catholic teaching and practice is the evolution of the idea of *justice*. When the bishops at Vatican II proclaimed that peace "is rightly and appropriately called 'an enterprise of justice'" (*GS* 78; see Isaiah 32:7), it was with a particular view of justice in mind. It was biblical justice. The biblical idea is rooted, as is so much of Israelite thought, in the experience of covenant. The fundamental reality for the pious Jew was that Yahweh had freely entered into a relationship with the Jewish people that was marked by God's faithful and devoted love *(hesed)*. In those times when that fidelity and devotion was reciprocated by the Israelites, the experience of covenant was that the Jewish people lived in a set of right relationships—with God, one another, and

6. Robert McElroy, "Why We Must Withdraw From Iraq," *America* (April 30, 2007).

creation. *Justice* was the term used to characterize this state of being in right relationship.

Biblical justice is of a different nature than what Americans think of as justice. Unlike the American idea of justice as impartial or "blind," the biblical concept of justice portrays Yahweh as being partial, with a clear bias in favor of the Jewish people in general and with the poor and marginal a particular object of divine favor. This explains the prophets' regular citation of the widow, orphan, and alien as a test of the community. This biblical triad represents those people most at risk in a patriarchal and tribal society. In such a society, women and children without a spouse or father and aliens without kinship relations are understood as people on the margins of the community. So the test of a community's justice is whether those who might be easily neglected are instead brought into right relationship with others.

In modern Catholic teaching, this biblical perspective of justice informs the way that the Church understands social justice. Community is at the heart of the Catholic vision of justice; the goal is establishing communities where people are able to live in right relationship with one another as well as with God and the rest of creation. Creating communal institutions and policies that reach out to and protect the marginal in modern societies is a key test of justice. When Catholic social teaching discusses a preferential option for the poor, it is simply trying to retrieve the biblical idea of a special love and concern for those people who represent the contemporary version of widows, orphans, and aliens in our societies.

When the bishops at Vatican II declared, "Peace results from that harmony built into human society by its divine Founder, and actualized by persons as they thirst after ever greater justice,"[7] they presumed an appreciation of the tradition they followed. This text presents not only the communitarian perspective of justice found in the Bible, but also the Augustinian theme of an order of tranquillity that eventuates from harmonious relationships.

It is with the above background that one can properly interpret Pope Paul VI's famous statement that dubbed development as "the new name for peace."[8] When Paul surveyed the state of the globe in the late 1960s, he concluded that the great social question of the time was the growing

7. Vatican II, Pastoral Constitution *(Gaudium et Spes)*, 78.
8. Pope Paul VI, On the Development of Peoples (*Populorum Progressio*), 76.

gap between rich and poor, both within states and between them. The gap is economic but also political as many experience a degree of powerlessness that prevents them from bringing about beneficial change.

For Pope Paul VI, the needed remedy was assisting the poor to undergo integral development, an approach not limited to the economic realm but inclusive of all dimensions of human well-being. An important aspect of such a holistic view of development is that the poor and marginal must be active agents of their advancement. What is needed is not a paternalistic charity that maintains the poor as passive objects of concern, but empowerment that enables them to participate in their development.

Justice as participation has become an important emphasis of Catholic social teaching. It suggests both the goal of justice as full participation in the life of a community, and the means to that goal, the empowerment of the poor as active agents. So "development" as the new name for peace must be understood as a certain kind of development, one that is both just and participatory.

An additional nuance that can be added to this evolving understanding of peace as just and participatory development came twenty years after Pope Paul VI wrote his encyclical. In 1987, John Paul II, reflecting on Paul's teaching, issued a second encyclical on development stating that solidarity is "the path to peace and at the same time to development."[9] Solidarity provides an energy that fosters a desire to work toward a truly just and participatory development. From this work of solidarity in the pursuit of development will emerge genuine peace. "The goal of peace, so desired by everyone, will certainly be achieved through the putting into effect of social and international justice, but also through the practice of virtues which favor togetherness, and which teach us to live in unity."[10]

To summarize these comments on the evolution of Catholic thinking on peace, it is the outcome of a committed engagement (solidarity) to the project of social progress for individuals and societies (just and participatory development). The modern papacy has promoted this understanding by linking *development* as the new term for *peace* and solidarity as the crucial step in working for a just development. Solidar-

9. Pope John Paul II, On Social Concern *(Sollicitudo Rei Socialis)*, 39. It adds a further nuance to the Catholic teaching on *development* as the name for peace.
10. Ibid., 39.

ity is the path to development, and peace is the end result of working for a development that is integral, just, and participatory.

Catholic thought on war and peace has moved through stages where pacifism and then just war theories were dominant. Recently, there has been a restoration of pacifism as a legitimate moral option and a refinement of just war theory, in the face of modern warfare, to see it as establishing a presumption against war. At the same time, there has been a strong trend to link peace to a particular form of justice, one that addresses the need for overcoming the inequalities that undermine human community.

A New Emphasis: Peacebuilding

With this background one can see why the Catholic tradition has become more and more interested in what is called *peacebuilding.* The just war tradition has focused on war avoidance or war limitation and the pacifist tradition on opposition to war. Peacebuilding takes a different tack and focuses attention on conditions for creating peace. It presumes, in agreement with the Catholic tradition, that peace is something positive, not simply the absence of violence. As such, strategies to establish peace and advance its maturation can be devised and promoted.

Catholic social teaching does not focus on peacebuilding expressly, but it does contain a good deal of discussion about peace and what it means. Peacebuilding is implied whenever Catholic teaching talks about justice, and in the recent papal teaching a particular form of justice—development.

The multiple levels of development demand that peacebuilding be understood broadly. Indeed, while some in the policy community identify several distinct tasks, the Catholic tradition stresses the way that the different tasks are related modes of working for peace and not separate stages that are hermetically sealed off from each other.

First, there is the realm of what can be called *prevention,* that is, identifying situations that might produce conflict and then through diplomacy removing the sources of violent before it erupts. A second concern entails *peacemaking,* efforts to resolve issues that have already led to conflict. Yet another task is *peacekeeping,* working to preserve fragile ceasefires or interim solutions in order to create space for implementing agreed-upon measures to achieve a lasting change in tense relations. And finally, there is *building peace* by means of renewing institutions and infrastructure destroyed by war, encouraging actions of mutual benefit to opposing groups, and addressing the larger cause of conflict found in economic, social, and political injustice.

The "Four Ps"—prevention, peacemaking, peacekeeping, and peacebuilding—have been given further clarification in an important U.N. report issued in the early 1990s. There one finds terms defined this way:

- Preventive diplomacy is action to prevent disputes from arising between parties, to prevent existing disputes from escalating into conflicts and to limit the spread of the latter when they occur.
- Peacemaking is action to bring hostile parties to agreement, essentially through such peaceful means as those foreseen in Chapter VI of the Charter of the United Nations.
- Peacekeeping is the deployment of a United Nations presence in the field, hitherto with the consent of all the parties concerned, normally involving United Nations military and/or police personnel and frequently civilians as well.[11]

In a separate paragraph the report refers to peacebuilding as a "concept" that is "critically related" to the above terms; it is understood to address "postconflict" issues, including "action to identify and support structures which will tend to strengthen and solidify peace in order to avoid a relapse into conflict."[12] Simply put, peacebuilding follows successful efforts at preventive diplomacy, peacemaking, and peacekeeping; it is aimed at halting recurrence of violence. This way of understanding peacebuilding, as a distinct and separate stage, is but one way that the term is often used.

Besides the UN-influenced usage, another more inclusive version of peacebuilding is used by many workers in nongovernmental organizations (NGOs). This second understanding proposes that peacebuilding subsumes peacemaking and peacekeeping. "In this view, peacebuilding includes early warning and response efforts, violence prevention, advocacy work, civilian and military peacekeeping, military intervention, humanitarian assistance, ceasefire agreements, and the establishment

11. Boutros Boutros-Ghali, *An Agenda for Peace* (New York: United Nations, 1992), no. 20.
12. Ibid., no. 21.

of peace zones."[13] This broader sense is closer to how Catholic activists and theorists use the term. Peacebuilding embraces both short- and longer-term strategies at transforming existing situations that either may lead to violent conflict or have already resulted in such conflict.

Even as the emphasis on the proactive strategies for peacebuilding grows within Catholic thought on war and peace, there is a willingness to consider that the just war tradition continues to have relevance. In particular, there has been a recognition that armed force may be necessary to remove certain obstacles to peace, even if military force cannot be the sole cause of securing peace. The clearest illustration of the ongoing support for just war thinking within the Church's teaching is the support expressed for what is called *humanitarian intervention.* The utility of military force to repel naked aggression against innocents, or to depose oppressive regimes engaged in extreme human rights violations such as genocide, continues to find support in Catholic social teaching.

Another aspect of the just war tradition is the convergence between peacebuilding and what has come to be called the *jus post bellum* [justice after war] category in just war theory. Traditionally, just war theory has been divided into two categories of concerns. The *jus ad bellum* addressed the question of when it was appropriate to go to war, under what conditions. *Jus in bello* took up questions of how to fight war, what strategies and tactics were morally defensible, and what did not count as fighting fair. During the past fifteen years or so, a new set of concerns has arisen: how to end a war and what moral duties are incumbent on combatants after a war is over.

This last set of concerns falls under a new heading, *jus post bellum.* Some interpretations of the rights and duties after war only address a narrow range of issues such as war crimes or war reparations. But a more expansive view of *post bellum* obligations takes up issues of rebuilding and restoring infrastructure that are not only physical, for example, bridges and power grids, but also political and social, such as forms of government, legal systems, and educational institutions. The presumption is that any attempt to return to the status quo before the war is neither possible—war is too destructive—nor wise since, after

13. Michelle Maiese, "What It Means to Build a Lasting Peace" posted on Beyond Intractability.org (www.beyondintractability.org/essay/peacebuilding) in September 2003 (accessed July 16, 2007).

all, the status quo is what led to the conflict at the outset. Instead, what is needed is an effort to create a better situation than had existed prior to the war. This is especially the case in humanitarian intervention where the avowed motive for the war was not to punish an aggressor nation but to assist an oppressed people in attaining a more humane life.

Seen in this way, developments in the just war tradition would appear to be moving in the same direction as the interest in peacebuilding with its aim of bringing about social transformation for the sake of avoiding conflict or restoring societies after conflict. However, thorny questions also accompany these developments. What changes and what level of assistance are moral duties for victors in war? In cases of civil war or intrastate conflicts, can the pursuit of justice in the face of war crimes exacerbate postconflict tensions to the point that peacebuilding is less likely? What are the duties of an occupying force? What degree of ongoing intervention in the internal life of a people is justified by peacebuilding? Can outsiders demand political change that is not endorsed by large segments of the population? These questions suggest that, as helpful as the category may be, *jus post bellum* also creates a new set of issues about which thoughtful and fair-minded citizens can disagree.

Conclusion

For a tradition to be a living tradition it must have a "growing end." While rooted in the past, it must engage the circumstances of the present. A living tradition permits not only the wisdom of the past to inform our response to the present, but for the present to elicit development in the tradition itself as it encounters new settings and new questions.

Clearly, a process of development has been under way in Catholic thinking about peace. Building on the ancient wisdom of the Scriptures and the patristic writers, there has been further reflection on the nature of justice as it leads to peace. Justice, characterized by participation and solidarity, is what helps to bring about authentic development; and development is the new name for peace. A renewed appreciation for pacifism and nonviolence as strategies for advancing true peace is also notable. Within the just war tradition itself, the establishment of a presumption against war as part of Catholic teaching and the emergence of the *jus post bellum* are additional indications of ongoing change. Finally, the new emphasis on peacebuilding, which hearkens back to the traditional claim that peace is positive and not simply the absence of violence, gives additional evidence that Catholic teaching continues to evolve on the topics of peace and war.

Informed by all these new insights, dedicated disciples and faithful citizens can join with our Church's leaders in addressing the difficult challenges that stand before us as American Catholics. In their reflection on those challenges, the bishops posed a series of questions, including the following related to the topic of working for peace:

> *After September 11, how can we build not only a safer world, but a better world—more just, more secure, more peaceful, more respectful of human life and dignity?...*
>
> *How will our nation pursue the values of justice and peace in a world where injustice is common, desperate poverty widespread, and peace is too often overwhelmed by violence?...*
>
> *When should our nation use, or avoid the use of, military force—for what purpose, under what authority, and at what human cost?*
>
> *How can we join with other nations to lead the world to greater respect for human life and dignity, religious freedom and democracy, economic justice, and care for God's creation?*[14]

Clearly these are tough questions that will create debates among serious and committed Church members. What seems beyond dispute, however, is that Catholics have an obligation to confront these questions using the wisdom of our moral tradition to assist us in forming our answers and deciding our actions. By doing so, we will take seriously the words of our Lord, "Blessed are the peacemakers, for they will be called children of God" (Matthew 5:9).

14. USCCB, "Faithful Citizenship" (2003), Part II. "Tasks and Questions for Believers," 4–6.

6. Protection of Life: Priorities and Politics

Lisa Sowle Cahill, Ph.D., Boston College

In his paper, Richard Miller eloquently addresses the responsibility of Catholic leaders and voters to advocate for a variety of human and social goods that are essential to the protection of life. He reminds us that while abortion may be one of the most visible issues defining Catholic political participation, it is one issue on an interrelated spectrum of issues. In fact, "Faithful Citizenship" calls for Catholic political commitment on no less than fifty issues, among them welfare reform, child tax credits, affordable housing, and universal health insurance.[1] Issues such as these, of course, are also very relevant to families and especially pregnant women.

Miller rightly points out that criminalization of abortion does not in fact correlate with its prevention or even reduction. He cites statistics from countries in Western Europe with low abortion rates (Belgium, Germany, and the Netherlands) to show that even where abortion is legal and available, it is not widely used if contraception education is also available. I would like to emphasize another point that follows from the same data, and that is the strong correlation of low abortion rates with the availability of economic and social support programs for women, children, and families. In other words, there is a positive correlation between poverty and abortion. Statistics show high rates of abortion in Peru, Chile, and Brazil, Catholic countries where abortion is illegal, where maternal death rates are high, and where poverty is also significant.

I want to argue that "protection of life" requires a vigorous social ethics and ethics of the common good. In other words, the three issue categories of "Faithful Citizenship"—protection of life, family life, and social justice—are always interrelated. It is not possible to achieve success in one without the others. As did traditional moral theology, we Catholics still see life issues too much in terms of individual rights, decisions, and responsibilities and too little in terms of the responsibility that all of us have as a society to put in place truly effective

1. United States Conference of Catholic Bishops, "Faithful Citizenship: A Catholic Call to Political Responsibility" (Washington, DC: United States Conference of Catholic Bishops, 2003), front matter.

institutions that not only protect life, but make dignified human life possible. Life issues are not just matters of personal ethics and/or of laws restricting personal decisions—they are very important matters of our Catholic commitment to the common good and to a good society. And I will stress that the protection of life demands that we do better at addressing poverty, sexism, and racism.

First, I will spend a bit more time with that most politically vexing of issues, abortion, and then draw just a few of the bishops' other fifty issues into the picture. In particular, I will highlight one issue on which Catholicism's public profile needs to be greatly magnified: the death penalty. In The Gospel of Life *(Evangelium Vitae)*, Pope John Paul II condemned both abortion and the death penalty as part of a "culture of death."[2]

I believe that the prevalence of abortion in our society and the fact that we are the only modern, Western, democratic country to kill people convicted of crimes are both symptoms of three basic cultural failings. First, we want simple, immediate, clear, and easy solutions to complex human problems. Second, we prefer to see ourselves and others in simple terms—black and white, good and evil, insider and outsider. With regard to abortion, this translates into positions that focus exclusively either on the fetus or on the woman, to see one's own position as morally absolute, and to demonize opponents. In the case of the death penalty, condemning and killing "the guilty" gives us a sense of security both about our own moral rectitude and about whether we or our society can immunize ourselves against suffering and injustice. The third and biggest failing is our bias toward using violence to solve problems—again in a simple framework of right and wrong, just and unjust, and with no gray areas.

Part of my argument on protection of life will be that certain tactics that Catholics have for "prioritizing" life issues need to be rethought, if not discarded. I am thinking of the role of certain traditional distinctions, often associated with the use of the principle of double effect. For example, it is sometimes said that the duty to defend innocent life is absolute, while the lives of the "guilty" have lost their sacred dignity. It is sometimes claimed that we have personal responsibility for lives we "directly" destroy but not for lives whose destruction we merely

2. Pope John Paul II, The Gospel of Life *(Evangelium Vitae)*. Vatican City: Libreria Editrice Vaticana, March 23, 1995.

"tolerate." The principle behind protection of life is deceptively simple: "It is always wrong directly to take an innocent human life." Hence, we are responsible for embryos and patients in a "persistent vegetative state," but we are not responsible for premature death caused by lack of health insurance, for deaths of civilians in Iraq, for infant mortality due to global poverty, or for villagers who die in floods caused by global warming. Also dismissed as "indirect" victims are wrongly convicted prisoners on death row—or young men who have in fact committed crimes but who are also products of a racist society that punishes unwed mothers, has a class-based public education system, exploits low-wage workers, and makes a general practice of rationalizing violence while denying personal blame.

Distinctions between the innocent and guilty, and between direct and indirect intentions and actions have their place, but they are no longer adequate. They are too often simplistic. They may even be morally self-deceptive—in light of the Catholic commitment to the common good, and of the gospel mandate to love our neighbor (and even enemy) and to live in solidarity with the poor.

The keynote for the protection of life is well established by the introduction to "Faithful Citizenship" (written by the general secretary of the USCCB, Msgr. William P. Fay). It calls every Catholic to make a public witness to "the Church's commitment to human life and dignity with special preference for the poor and vulnerable." The introduction identifies the key idea for an election year as the common good. The bishops intend that the common good include the dignity and well-being of every member of society. Hence, the "central questions" they ask are, "How can 'we'—all of us, especially the weak and vulnerable—be better off in the years ahead? How can we protect and promote human life and dignity? How can we pursue greater justice and peace?....Who has a place at the table of life?"[3]

In May 2007, the USCC Department of Social Development and World Peace sent a message to Congress called "Poverty in the Midst of Plenty." The bishops pose the question, "How are we to treat 'the least among us' in our nation and our world?" They answer, "The moral measure of our society must be how we care for the weak and neglected." Mindful of "Americans without health care, the many children

3. Ibid., 2.

who go to bed hungry and the millions of parents who work every day, but cannot provide a decent future for their children," the bishops urge that Congress prioritize assistance for low-income families, opposition to the death penalty, health and education aid to sub-Saharan Africa, debt reduction for the world's poorest countries, and termination of sanctions against Cuba that hurt only the poor.

The bishops echo the political framework established by Pope John Paul II, who "told an American audience in 2000 that the poverty of billions of men, women and children is 'the one issue that most challenges our human and Christian consciences.'"[4] In fact, when in 2001, President George W. Bush consulted the pope on stem cell research, he warned the president of the dangers of creating research embryos, abortion, euthanasia, and infanticide. But these problems were neither his first nor his central concern. Instead, he devoted the majority of his remarks to divisions between rich and poor. He told the president, "Respect for human dignity and belief in the equal dignity of all the members of the human family demand policies aimed at enabling all peoples to have access to the means required to improve their lives...."[5]

The Pope's emphasis on the just use of medical resources underlines the message that all life issues must be seen in light of the common good, not as isolated cases. We miss this if we talk about stem cell research only in terms of embryos, of abortion only in terms of the unborn, and of capital punishment only in terms of the guilty. In fact, in my view, the misappropriation of medical resources is the *primary* moral objection to funding of stem cell research. This problem will not be overcome by new techniques of creating stem cells without using embryos. When 47 million people in our own country lack health insurance, and when millions are dying around the globe from preventable or treatable diseases such as AIDS, malaria, and tuberculosis, it is highly questionable whether a top priority for public research funding should be therapies for First-World diseases that will be marketed only to the rich or the well-insured. If we fail to see this, then we are very short-sighted compared to the late pope.

---

4. Catholics in Alliance for the Common Good (http://www.catholicsinalliance.org/), *Voting for the Common Good: A Practical Guide for Conscientious Catholics* (Washington, DC: Catholics in Alliance for the Common Good, 2006), 8.
5. "Remarks by John Paul," *The New York Times*, July 24, 2001, A8.

Seeing protection of life through the poverty lens, let us return to the problem of abortion. There is a connection internationally between abortion and poverty. That connection also holds true for abortion rates in the United States specifically. Abortion rose sharply after its legalization in 1973, but by the early 1980s had begun a decline that has lasted for twenty years. During the Bush administrations, that decline has slowed almost to a standstill. Confirmatory statistics are provided by the Alan Guttmacher Institute, a nonprofit organization whose data are cited by all sides in the abortion debate. Half of all pregnancies among American women are unintended, and most of these (four of five) end in abortion. (This point underscores Rich Miller's suggestion that contraceptive education might be a very effective tactic to fight abortion.) Overall unintended pregnancy rates have stagnated over the past decade.[6] Yet, since 1994, unintended pregnancy increased by 29 percent among poor women while decreasing 20 percent among higher-income women. Women who are "economically disadvantaged" are more likely to choose abortion (57 percent). Lower-income women also have abortions later in pregnancy, at least partly because of difficulty in securing funds. Restrictions such as waiting periods and parental notification laws do not reduce the overall incidence of resort to abortion,[7] but access to social support systems does reduce abortion.

A pilot study on the link between poverty and abortion in Kansas was conducted by Catholics United for the Common Good, a social justice organization that works with progressive Catholic groups such as NETWORK, A National Catholic Social Justice Lobby. The data from Kansas are significant because Kansas is a typical state with regard to abortion. Abortion rates are similar to national averages; public opinion on abortion is fairly evenly split; and abortion politics in Kansas are public and divisive. The study compared 2000–2004 data from different counties and concluded that economic disadvantages encourage abortion. The evidence indicates that jobs, opportunities for children such as Head Start programs, and health insurance coverage exert a downward influence on abortion rates. This is true even from county

6. Alan Guttmacher Institute: "In Brief: Facts on Induced Abortion in the United States" (www.alanguttmacher.org/pubs/fb_induced_abortion.html; accessed 6/13/07).

7. Rebecca West, "News Release, A Tale of Two Americas for Women: Low-Income Women's Unplanned Pregnancy and Abortion Rates Are Increasing as Better-Off Women Continue Three Decades of Progress," Alan Guttmacher Institute, May 4, 2006 (www.guttmacher.org/media/nr/2006/05/05/index.html; accessed June 13, 2007).

to county in Kansas, although unemployment rates vary dramatically. In Kansas, the population most lacking health insurance consists of working adults with low incomes, not the unemployed, who qualify for public assistance.[8]

Obviously, this sends a message with regard to Catholic political priorities and the interconnection of all life issues. America needs to invest in child care and education; universal health insurance should be on the agenda of all Catholics as a priority; and justice-based immigration reform is essential. Many immigrants lack not only adequate employment and health insurance but even access to the minimal support net for mothers and children that this country provides for citizens.

I want to emphasize and develop the point that Catholic advocacy for the dignity and rights of women is essential to the credibility of the Catholic message about protection of life. Earlier I suggested that the traditional analysis of "direct" abortion as a mortal sin, along with the relegation of social causes of abortion to a realm of lesser moral significance, was an outdated and even morally delinquent analysis of the issues. Social justice for women must be part of any effective approach to the morality and politics of abortion. The typical Catholic analysis of abortion is reflected in *The Ethical and Religious Directives for Catholic Health Care Services*, which states "Abortion (that is, the directly intended termination of pregnancy before viability or the directly intended destruction of a viable fetus) is never permitted."[9] Pope John Paul II, in his 1995 Letter to Women, calls abortion even after rape "a grave sin." Yet he does not stop there. Abortion may be a grave sin, but it is also a social sin. The pope attributes this sin *not* primarily to women seeking to terminate pregnancies, even though they are the ones traditionally accused of "direct attack on innocent life." He attributes the sin of abortion to irresponsible and violent male behavior, and to "the complicity of the general social environment" that approves aggression toward women.[10] This same political environ-

---

8. Joseph Wright, "Reducing Abortion in Kansas: Expanding Jobs and Health Insurance for Families and Opportunities for Children," August 1, 2006, sponsored by the Catholic Voting Project (www.votingcatholic.org) of Catholics United for the Common Good (www.catholics-united.org).

9. *Ethical and Religious Directives for Catholic Health Care Services,* 4th ed. (Washington, DC: United States Conference of Catholic Bishops, 2001) no. 45, www.usccb.org/bishops/directives.shtml; accessed 6/13/07.

10. Pope John Paul II, Letter to Women (Vatican City: Libreria Editrice Vaticana, 1995), 5.

ment excludes many women from necessary resources to raise healthy children. It is clear why the pope immediately goes on to commend women who have "devoted their lives to...fighting for their basic social, economic and political rights."

In my view, the greatest obstacle to wider appreciation of the Catholic Church's "pro-life" message on abortion is its too-frequent silence on the social, economic, and political rights of women, as well as women's rights in the family, marriage, and maternity—all of which have been affirmed by Pope John Paul II, and in recent Catholic social teaching. The late pope's appreciation of women was couched in a gender-complementarity model that many find limiting to women's true equality. Yet, there is no doubt that he affirmed women's rights in employment, political participation, access to social benefits, and self-determination in the areas of sex and reproduction.[11] But these rights are all too rarely part of the pro-life message. Fortunately, some Catholics, especially women, do offer exceptions to this norm—for example, the advocacy group Feminists for Life, and the author and former *Commonweal* columnist Sidney Callahan.

Angela Senander, a pro-life feminist and moral theology professor at the Washington Theological Union, conducted a survey a few years ago that revealed the ambivalence of the Catholic commitment to support young women with unplanned pregnancies. In 2004, Senander followed up a statement of Jesuit provincials supporting the unborn by investigating the actual levels of support offered to pregnant students by Jesuit colleges and universities. She found that only seven schools offered pregnancy tests, four offered counseling, two offered campus ministry resources, and one referred students to a women's center. Only two offered the possibility of deferring student loans. Georgetown and Marquette did better than the others by organizing and publicizing a variety of services through a single Web site. Yet, no campuses offered financial assistance during pregnancy, housing alternatives, or child care.[12]

Why is it that the "pro-life" message so often neglects women's needs and rights in favor of a one-sided emphasis on the rights of the unborn? Why is it that the U.S. bishops' excellent 1992 pastoral letter

11. See also John Paul II, On the Family *(Familiaris Consortio,* 1981). Vatican City: Libreria Editrice Vaticana, 1982), 22–24.

12 .Angela Senander, "Standing With Pregnant Students," *America*, May 24, 2004; available at www.americamagazine.org.

on domestic abuse, *When I Call for Help: Domestic Violence Against Women*,[13] is not as well known in church or society as Catholic condemnations of unwed pregnancy, pregnancy termination, or even gay marriage? When the Church downplays ecclesial, social, and political support for women, and the full equality of women, it undermines its own message that the welfare of women and children is important, and that the protection of the lives of both is a political priority and a responsibility of the common good. If the Catholic Church were as visible in its support of nondiscriminatory policies toward women in education, employment, child care, and family benefits as it is visible in its opposition to abortion, its pro-life message would be more honest, transparent, and respected.

A recent, glaring example of failure in this regard is a June 2007 call by the Vatican for all Catholics to cease support of Amnesty International because the human rights organization had called for an end to legal penalties for women who have abortions, and its defense of abortion as an option for women who are victims of sexual violence or incest, or whose pregnancies endanger their health. Amnesty defended its actions as part of its international campaign to combat violence against women and to reduce the number of women (68,000) who die annually from illegal abortions.

Instead of applauding and joining efforts to end domestic and sexual violence, the president of the Vatican's Pontifical Council for Justice and Peace chose to respond merely that "abortion is murder," that it kills an "innocent child," and that it cannot be justified, even in the event of rape. Given realities such as gang rape of women in war and frequent ostracization of women who have been sexually violated, this was hardly an effective way to communicate the fullness of the "gospel of life." How much more effective Catholic advocacy for life would have been had the response focused first and foremost on the Catholic commitment to defend all life, and especially its agreement with Amnesty's fundamental goal of protecting women's human rights, even if not with abortion as a means.[14]

---

13. USCCB Committees on Women in Church and Society, and on Marriage and Family Life: "When I Call for Help: Domestic Violence Against Women," *Origins* 22/21 (1992): 353, 355–358.

14. "Vatican Tells Catholics to Abandon Amnesty," *The Australian*, 14 June (2007) (www.theaustralian.news.come.au/story/0.20867.21904009-2703.00.html; accessed June 15, 2007).

Advocacy for women is key to successful pro-life advocacy. This is especially true because most Americans, including Catholics, do not agree with a key premise of the Church's single-minded opposition to abortion: the moral equivalence of all life from conception to so-called natural death.[15] Pro-life Catholics committed to this view have a duty in conscience to try to persuade others of its truth. Nevertheless, it is obvious to most people that women have more rights than fetuses do. Many people are ambivalent about how much protection is owed human life before birth, especially when it is a danger to its mother. In a recent Internet discussion of the threat of some bishops to excommunicate "pro-choice" politicians, one participant wrote the following heartfelt message:

> *Is anyone willing to raise any kind of question about the growing tendency to call the abortion of an embryo the murder of an unborn child? Can we not even ask our bishops and cardinals to explain why (the) distinction between abortion (of a fetus) and murder (killing of an adult) no longer (has) a place in church language? Do we all believe it is an act of murder for a woman who is pregnant as the result of a rape to have an abortion?*

Although there are undoubtedly Catholic theologians, bishops, and even politicians who are willing to answer that question in the affirmative, it seems highly unlikely to me that disagreement on this issue will be overcome in our society as a whole any time soon, if ever. In fact, if there is a public consensus in the United States, it is currently around the perception that an embryo is *not* morally the same as a baby or child, even though embryos and fetuses deserve protection and respect. This presses the question whether people who disagree on this point can still find ways to work together to reduce abortions now.

Any serious, credible, and potentially effective political approach to abortion must appeal to the majority in our culture who do not agree with the "Catholic" position on the status of the embryo and fetus. I

---

15. In my view, this term is a misnomer, for what Catholicism wants to protect is not "natural" death, but life that is valued as having intrinsic worth no matter what its condition. If a "natural" death were the issue, we would not approve life-extending medical technologies. Rather, what we are or should be interested in, is always seeking the dignity of the person, while not forgetting the demands of the "common good," as including families, other potential recipients of health resources, and the resources of local communities.

personally doubt that the recriminalization of abortion is a politically and practically feasible goal. To achieve concrete results, Catholics must define goals that can command broad social support. Catholics must persuade politicians and voters that abortion, which few see as an optimal choice anyway, can be avoided through alternatives that provide genuinely more successful and satisfying ways for women to contend with problematic pregnancies or to avoid such pregnancies altogether. Those alternatives require advocacy for women and against poverty.

Some measures before Congress offer promise in this direction. The Pregnant Women Support Act aims to reduce the abortion rate by 95 percent over ten years by addressing the root causes of abortion: poverty, lack of affordable health care, and job security. Introduced by Congressman Lincoln David (D-TN) in September 2006, this bipartisan effort has joined pro-choice and pro-life members of Congress. A key provision is a ban on the current discriminatory practice of the health insurance industry of defining pregnancy as a "pre-existing condition" that disqualifies a woman from obtaining health care coverage. Other provisions are informed consent for abortion services, requiring State Children's Health Insurance Programs (SCHIPs) to cover pregnant women and their unborn children, making adoption tax credits permanent, providing grants for low-income parenting college students, fully funding the federal food program Women, Infants, and Children (WIC), increasing funding for domestic violence programs, and providing free home visits to new mothers by visiting nurses. This so-called 95/10 initiative has been endorsed by groups including Democrats for Life of America (www.democratsforlife.org) and Catholics in Alliance for the Common Good, a bipartisan social justice organization that has as its mission the promotion of an integrated Catholic common good approach to politics and voting (www.catholicsinalliance.org).

Support for broad life-protecting measures among Catholic leaders may be easy to obtain, at least in theory. But the test of our genuine "pro-life" commitment is willingness to shine a very public light of approval and encouragement on steps to protect both women and children, steps that empower women in their own right as mothers and as members of society. A truly "pro-life" commitment demands a broad-based political strategy that demonstrates the willingness of Catholics to work together with others for progress toward the common good and the dignity of all persons.

The common good and the dignity of persons make it impossible to accept that killing of any sort is a customary act, protected within our basic social institutions. This includes capital punishment, which in our country is a racist practice. Catholic theology, going back to Augustine and Aquinas, does permit the exceptional killing of human beings, in cases of extreme emergency and immediate threat to life. Hence, we accept killing in war or in humanitarian interventions as sometimes a tragic necessity; the same is true in some cases of pregnancy and self-defense. However, the position of the Church today is that in most societies and circumstances, capital punishment is *not* a necessary last resort.

In 1999, here in St. Louis, Pope John Paul II called the "followers of Christ" to be "unconditionally pro-life," and to recognize that the dignity of life must never be taken away, even when someone is guilty of "great evil." Rehabilitation, and not retribution, retaliation or vengeance, is the appropriate purpose of punishment (Rome, 2002). John Paul II repudiated "the unnecessary recourse to the death penalty 'when other bloodless means are sufficient to defend human lives against an aggressor and to protect public order and the safety of persons. Today, given the means at the state's disposal to deal with crime and control those who commit it without abandoning all hope of their redemption, the cases where it is absolutely necessary to do away with an offender 'are now very rare, even nonexistent practically' " (On the Encounter With the Living Jesus Christ: The Way to Conversion, Communion and Solidarity in America *[Ecclesia in America]*).[16] The *Compendium of the Social Doctrine of the Church* confirms these views and commends the "heightened moral awareness" of movements and societies that are working to abolish the death penalty.[17]

Civilized peoples see the death penalty as a violation of human rights; more than half the countries in the world—133—have abolished the death penalty in law or in practice. The vast majority of executions

16. These quotations are taken from "Statements on the Death Penalty by the Holy Father," published on the Web site of Catholic Campaign to End the Use of the Death Penalty, United States Conference of Catholic Bishops (www.usccb.org/sdwp/national/deathpenalty/holyfather.shtml; accessed 6/12/07).
17. See the *Compendium of the Social Doctrine of the Church* (Washington, DC: USCCB, 2005), nos. 405, 833–836, also cited on the Web site of Catholic Campaign to End the Use of the Death Penalty, United States Conference of Catholic Bishops (www.usccb.org/sdwp/national/deathpenalty/compendium.shtml; accessed 6/12/07).

worldwide are carried out in a handful of countries. In 2006, 91 percent of all known executions took place in six: China, Iran, Pakistan, Iraq, Sudan, and the United States. In 2005, after a half-century of increasingly restrictive policies on the death penalty, the U.N. Commission on Human Rights called for all nations that still maintain the death penalty to abolish it completely and, in the meantime, to place a moratorium on executions.[18]

Unfortunately, public moral sentiment in the United States does not yet reflect "heightened awareness" of the evil of state-sanctioned killing. More than one thousand people were put to death in the United States over the past three decades. Dozens had histories of serious mental illness, either preceding the crimes for which they were convicted or at the time of their execution. More than two-thirds of executions occurred in just five states: Texas (over three times more than any other state), Virginia, Oklahoma, Missouri, and Florida. Nearly half of death row inmates are black, although their percentage in the overall U.S. population is only about 13 percent.[19] According to Amnesty International, the death penalty in the United States is racially biased.

In a 1990 report, the nonpartisan U.S. General Accounting Office found "[A] pattern of evidence indicating racial disparities in the charging, sentencing, and imposition of the death penalty." The study concluded that a defendant was several times more likely to be sentenced to death if the murder victim was white. This confirms the findings of many other studies that, holding all other factors constant, the single most reliable predictor of whether someone will be sentenced to death is the race of the victim.[20]

More than 80 percent of the victims of those receiving the death sentence were white, although half of all victims of homicide are African Americans. One in three of those executed since 1977 are also African Americans, again vastly disproportionate to their 13-percent presence in the population. Yet, African Americans are not

---

18. Amnesty International, Death Penalty Defies International Human Rights Standards.

19. United States Conference of Catholic Bishops, *A Culture of Life and the Penalty of Death* (Washington, DC: USCCB, 2005), 7. (www.usccb.org/sdwp/national/deathpenalty/index.shtml; accessed 6/12/07).

20. Amnesty International Web site, http://www.amnestyusa.org/abolish/racialprejudices.html; accessed 6/14/07.

responsible for a third of capital crimes, as is shown by the fact that inmates on death row are frequently found to be innocent, sometimes only after they have been executed. A 2002 Columbia University study that reviewed more than 4,000 capital cases over 23 years in 28 states, found 7 of every 10 death penalty cases contained serious errors. The fallibility of the U.S. legal system is acute with regard to the poor and racial minorities.[21]

Kirk Bloodsworth was the first capital conviction to be overturned in the United States as a result of DNA testing. After a long legal battle for a DNA test, crime scene evidence was reexamined. The final conclusion of state and federal labs was that Bloodsworth's DNA did not match any of the evidence. Ten years after his conviction was overturned, a DNA match was made to another man, who was convicted of the murder for which Bloodsworth was accused.

After spending almost nine years in prison (two on death row) after a wrongful conviction for the rape and murder of a child, Bloodsworth had this to say:

> *In that time, my life had been taken from me and destroyed....*
>
> *Every bit of my story exemplifies the problems in the death penalty system. The same systemic flaws that led to my wrongful conviction, such as mistaken identification, inadequate representation, prosecutorial misconduct, and basic human error, plague the cases of innocent people in prison and on death row.*[22]
>
> *The death penalty as it is actually enforced kills the innocent as well as perpetrators. "Its application is deeply flawed and can be irreversibly wrong, is prone to errors, and is biased by factors such as race, the quality of legal representation, and where the crime was committed."*[23]
>
> *Moreover, the death penalty is not only racist, classist, and fallible, it is ineffective. In the last 20 years, the homicide rate in*

---

21. Information on wrongful convictions is available at the Web site of The Justice Project. For the Columbia University study, see www.thejusticeproject.org/press/articles/protecting-the-accused.html; accessed July 10, 2007.
22. *A Culture of Life and the Penalty of Death*, 5.
23. *A Culture of Life and the Penalty of Death*, 3.

> *states with the death penalty has been 48 to 101 percent higher than in states without the death penalty.*[24]

In 2005, the U.S. bishops launched a campaign to abolish the death penalty (The Catholic Campaign to End the Use of the Death Penalty; http://www.usccb.org/sdwp/national/deathpenalty/index.shtml). In a new pastoral statement, *A Culture of Life and the Penalty of Death,* they assert that capital punishment diminishes all in societies in which it is practiced. Compassion and support for victims of violent crimes is an important ministry of the Church, and grave penalties for grave crimes are demanded by justice and the public order. However, systematic, institutionalized killing by the state does not accomplish these ends, and instead creates a generalized ethos of hatred, violence, and retaliation. According to the bishops, "No act, even an execution, can bring back a loved one or heal terrible wounds. The pain and loss of one death cannot be wiped away by another death."[25]

In *A Culture of Life and the Penalty of Death*, the U.S. Catholic bishops call the Catholic community to join in the campaign against the death penalty. We are told to advocate for better public policies, "to educate people in parishes, schools, religious education programs, universities, and seminaries" about Catholic teaching against the death penalty, and to "advocate in state legislatures, in the Congress, in the courts, and in the public square."[26] If this is so, my question is, "Why is opposition to the death penalty not a central, visible, vehemently reiterated, and publicly known part of the Catholic position on the 'protection of life'?" "Faithful Citizenship" mentions the death penalty in only one phrase. Why isn't this a defining Catholic issue, an "orthodoxy" issue, and a frontline Catholic voter issue?

One answer is certainly the bias in media coverage to select issues that play into the public's love of controversy around sex in general, and especially around seemingly reactionary or authoritarian religious positions. Catholic teaching on sex, gender, and reproduction is often perceived to fit this bill. There is no doubt a market for negative portrayals of Church teaching on sex and gender, and the media play

---

24. Amnesty International Web site, The Death Penalty Is Not a Deterrent, www.amnestyusa.org/Fact_Sheets/The_Death_Penalty_Is_Not_a_Deterrent/page.do?id=1101085&n1=3&n2=28&n3=99; citing a 2000 *New York Times* survey.
25. *A Culture of Life and the Penalty of Death*, 6.
26. Ibid., 17.

into this. However, I also detect a bias in the Catholic pro-life identity itself. As a group, bishops are just not as publicly active in advertising their position on capital punishment as they are on abortion—that is, the position that the rights of the unborn trump the needs of pregnant women. The campaign against recognition of gay unions is the only other issue that seems to enjoy anything like the support the anti-abortion platform receives from the "official" teachers of the Church. However, the blame does not end there or lie only on the side of social conservatives. More politically progressive theologians and Catholic leaders also tend to focus on the sex and gender issues and to select these issues as the focus of attacks on what progressives see as misguided Catholic leadership. Sex and gender are important issues, no doubt—but are they so disproportionately important that racism, war, immigration, health care reform, and global poverty are relegated to secondary status?

I conclude by emphasizing again that, as Catholics and Christians, we must always approach the protection of life through the lens of the common good and the preferential option for the poor. This lens reveals that one of the greatest threats to respect for life and to human dignity is poverty, usually in evil alliance with sexism and racism. Indeed, poverty is often due to discrimination on the basis of race, immigration status, and gender. To build a genuine culture of life, we must fight back against all the barriers to social participation and well-being that condemn human beings to a living death of non-personhood and marginalization, at home and abroad. We must make it not only a religious and ecclesial, but also a public and political, priority to raise our voices in favor of a good society. A good society provides for all the basic conditions of a dignified and fruitful life, and does so universally.

7. Catholic Environmentalism

Reverend Drew Christiansen, S. J., Ph.D., America *Magazine*

The Common Good Trumps "Takings" Legislation

> *Now the company of those who believed were of one heart and soul, and no one claimed private ownership of any possessions, but everything they owned was held in common* (Acts 4:32).

In January 1995, Newt Gingrich's Republican Revolution rolled into Washington. Its "Contract with America" aimed to remake the country.[1] Its ambitious goals entailed not only rolling back environmental legislation, but making future environmental regulation impossible. To carry out this plan, the congressional strategists had four proposals, which their alarmed critics dubbed "The Four Horsemen of the Apocalypse." Potentially the most damaging of these was "takings" legislation, an effort to expand the eminent domain clause of the Fifth Amendment, forbidding the taking of private property "for public use without just compensation."[2] Under this bill, property owners would have been able to sue the government for any loss in the potential market value of real property or in projected profits resulting from environmental legislation. If, for example, vacant property were designated wetland, the owner would then have been able to sue the government for the loss of the property, including the diminishment in its speculative value as development property; or if a power plant were required to reduce its atmospheric pollution, the owners could sue for the loss in profits due to the installation and use of the pollution-control mechanisms. It was not difficult to see that if the "takings" legislation had been enacted into law, environmental regulation would have come to a dead stop.

In late 1991, three years before the election of the One Hundred-Fourth Congress, the U.S. bishops had approved "Renewing the Earth," their pastoral statement on the environment. In 1993 the United States Catholic Conference (USCC), as it was then known, the National Council of Churches of Christ, the Evangelical Environmental Network, and

---

1. John Langan, S.J., "The Contract with America and Catholic Social Teaching," *America* 173, no. 3 (1995): 10–15.
2. See David DeCosse, "'Taking' Property and the Common Good," *America* 173, no. 2, 10–12.

the Coalition on the Environment and Jewish Life agreed to form the National Religious Partnership for the Environment. In September that year, the bishops' conference would inaugurate its own environmental justice program, designed to promote consciousness of the ecological crisis in parishes and dioceses and among Catholic educators, clergy, and leaders in social action.

Because of pressures inside and outside the conference, for a time major policy initiatives were limited to environmental justice, that is, issues where environment and poverty were obviously intertwined: for example, environmental health in poor communities and among children, so-called brownfields, and pollution along the U.S.-Mexican border. The religious community agreed that addressing the impact of environmental abuse on the poor was an area on which people of faith could have unique influence. More narrowly "green" issues, such as species extinction or climate change, were not regarded as actionable, at least in the short term, by the bishops. Confronted by "the Four Horsemen," the challenge facing the USCC staff was how to educate the bishops on complicated issues on which they had little expertise and on which their statements on complex issues of constitutional law might easily be questioned. Other members of the Partnership might announce immediate opposition to "takings"; the conference's only hope was to prepare for the long term. Even with strong congressional majorities, it often took years to get legislation passed.

Since the takings issue pitted property rights against environmental responsibility, as a first step we commissioned a paper on the relationship of private property and the common good from David DeCosse, now at Santa Clara University and then a graduate student at Boston College.[3] The paper's theme was "the social mortgage" on private property, that is, the social duties that limit the right to private property, as explained by Pope John Paul II in his two encyclical letters, On Human Work (*Laborem Exercens,* 1981) and in On Social Concern (*Sollicitudo Rei Socialis,* 1988).[4] While the Church has upheld private

3. See DeCosse above. The *America* article is a revision of the earlier draft prepared as a background paper for the USCC environmental justice program.

4. On the social mortgage, see Pope John Paul II, On Human Work *(Laborem Exercens),* nos. 52–58, and On Social Concern *(Sollicitudo Rei Socialis),* no. 42, in David J. O'Brien and Thomas A. Shannon, eds. *Catholic Social Thought: The Documentary Heritage* (Maryknoll, NY: Orbis, 1992). Also see "Compendium of the Social Doctrine of the Church" (Washington, DC: USCCB, Pontifical Council for Justice and Peace, 2005), nos. 176–184.

property as a means of defending the life and dignity of the person, it has, since the time of the Fathers of the Church, also held that property has a social function, to support and not impede the fundamental welfare of the rest of society.[5]

Applying this principle to environmental regulation, De Cosse wrote, the takings represented "a serious confusion of the categories of commutative and social justice." The first is the justice "of contracts"; the second deals with broader questions "of society and of politics."[6] David Hollenbach says that some rights are claims on goods that are essentially public and which cannot be weighed out and distributed piecemeal.[7] Examples of such public goods would be watersheds, marine fisheries, air quality, and unique landscapes, like Yosemite or the Grand Canyon.

As another example, in some Rocky Mountain states private landowners are forbidden from interrupting the flow of water through their land. The water is available for their use, but they must not take actions that would deprive others of use of the common water source, such as building dams and reservoirs. The proposed interpretation of "takings" would have permitted such private control of springs and creeks, and so have treated a good that is intrinsically shared as a private possession immune from public control.

Deborah Blake points to a related case of a conflict between the common good and private property deriving from an effort to divide historic communal water rights in the San Luis Valley in southern Colorado. Dating back to Spanish colonial times, the valley's mountain watershed had been held in common with water flowing to irrigate private holdings in the valley.[8] When one family "sold" its alleged "share" in the rights to an outside land company, the company proceeded to log timber from across the watershed, putting agriculture in the old land-

5. On the patristic teaching, see Charles Avila, *Ownership: Early Christian Teaching* (Maryknoll, NY: Orbis, 1983). For the decisive influence of the patristic ideas on contemporary teaching, see Vatican Council II, Pastoral Constitution on the Church in the Modern World *(Gaudium et Spes)* in *Catholic Social Thought*, 147. For a detailed overview of Catholic thinking on private property, see "Private Property" in Judith M. Dwyer, ed., *Dictionary of Catholic Social Thought* (Collegeville, MN: Liturgical Press, 1994), 785–790.
6. DeCosse, 12.
7. Cited in DeCosse, ibid.
8. Deborah D. Blake, "Toward a Sustainable Ethic: Virtue and the Environment" in Drew Christiansen, S.J., and Walter Grazer, eds., *"And God Saw It Was Good": Catholic Theology and the Environment* (Washington, DC: United States Catholic Conference, 1996), 201.

grant region at risk and leading to a legal conflict between the valley farmers and the purchaser. In sum, although everyone rightfully shares in the common good, it is not divisible. It is truly a commons owned by the whole community rather than by any individual or group.[9]

The staff reworked DeCosse's paper to address further the ongoing legislative debate and explain at greater length Catholic social teaching on the duties of private property. The revised paper was to have been a background piece for the two bishops' committees responsible for environmental policy (domestic and international policy). It would mark the beginning of the dialogue that might (or might not) result in policy recommendations by the committees. Somehow the Clinton White House learned about the paper before it had time to appear on a joint committee agenda. How, I still don't know. In any case, we got a request to provide the paper on a confidential basis. With caveats that the paper was completely unofficial—a "non-paper" as the diplomats say—we passed it along.

In what seemed like a very short time as Washington legislative calendars usually go, we got news the "takings" legislation was dead. The short version of the story is that Vice President Gore read the paper. He passed it to Senate Majority Leader Robert Dole. Dole read the paper and saw to it that the "takings" bill went no further. The following spring when members of the National Religious Partnership, led by Bishop Jim Malone of Youngstown, chair of the bishops' domestic policy committee and the lead on environmental issues, met with the vice president, the first thing Mr. Gore did after opening the meeting was to thank "the Catholics" for stopping the "takings" legislation.

I tell the story for three reasons. First, it shows the often overlooked and underestimated effectiveness of the bishops' conference on issues of public policy, and it illustrates how quiet, behind-the-scenes work can accomplish more than public hype. Second, it recalls the days when there was still bipartisan political comity in the capital. The Partnership

9. It is hard to project what arrangements might have been made for equitable compensation had the "takings" bill reached the floor. Historically the law of eminent domain had required that property owners be "made whole," but the use of sovereign immunity has curbed that right and prohibited suits against the government. In addition, in some states that immunity has been transferred to utility and railroad interests, and, as we saw in the New London case, the Supreme Court now backs taking of unblighted private land for entrepreneurial purposes under state immunity where the owner does not have to be made "whole," i.e., paid full value or other compensation (e.g., similar housing).

had worked with Mr. Gore on environmental issues. My first day on the job as director of the Office of International Justice and Peace at the bishops' conference, in fact, was spent at a meeting—convened at the American Museum of Natural History in New York by then-Senator Gore, the astronomer Carl Sagan, and National Council of Churches General Secretary Joan Brown Campbell—the Call of Science and Religion for the Environment—out of which grew the National Religious Partnership for the Environment. Later Senator Dole was also helpful, in a quiet but always decisive way, on a number of concerns of the conference, including the moratorium on antipersonnel landmines and humanitarian intervention in Bosnia. Obviously, the majority leader and the Senate president found they could work quietly behind the scenes for the common good. Finally, blocking "takings" is also one case I know when Catholic social teaching had a direct and speedy impact on the direction of American public policy. Usually effecting policy rooted in Catholic social teaching takes years of patient work to realize even a marginal impact on the law. Even in today's greener political climate with high public awareness of global warming, it will take patient effort to persuade the bishops, mobilize the Catholic faithful, and contribute to a serious change in public policy. In doing so, it is good to remember there have been important, unexpected victories in the recent past.

I. The Common Good: Bioregionalism and the Planetary Common Good

The earth is the LORD's and all that is in it;
the world, and those who live in it (Psalm 24:1).

One of the theological pillars of "Renewing the Earth" is the common good.[10] In discerning how they might define a distinctively Catholic participation in the environmental movement, the bishops believed that the Church with its universal scope was better suited than many environmental activists of the day to pursue environmental concerns that exceeded national boundaries. These included marine resources, such as fisheries, freshwater resources that supply more than one country, and the atmosphere, which nourishes the whole Earth. At the time,

10. "Renewing the Earth" in "And God Saw It Was Good," 223–243.

global warming was still a controversial issue, but ozone depletion was already a recognized ill for which the international community had found an agreed remedy: a complete ban on fluorocarbon aerosols known as the Montreal Protocol. One of the better examples of this stress on the common good was the Columbia River Pastoral, initiated with support from the U.S. bishops' environmental justice program. It involved twelve bishops, embracing four states (Washington, Oregon, Idaho, and Montana) and the Canadian province of British Columbia.[11] The letter dealt with the varied problems of the Columbia River Basin ranging from nuclear waste, to diminishing fish stocks, to the need for and problems of agricultural irrigation.

Another example of American Catholics' application of the common good to environmental issues was a series of initiatives on urban sprawl by Midwest dioceses. Beginning with Bishop Anthony M. Pilla's pastoral initiative, *The Church in the City* (2001), a series of dioceses circling the Great Lakes undertook early in this decade to address a host of environmental issues ranging from zoning to water quality, toxic waste, air quality, and transportation.[12] In several cases, these programs, like the Columbia River Pastoral, were honored by other, secular activists for their achievement.[13]

Both the Columbia River Pastoral and the Great Lakes sprawl programs were examples of *bioregionalism,* the movement that calls for addressing environmental problems across political boundaries in the natural zones in which they occur: in watersheds, like the Columbia River; or along migratory bird flyways that cross continents; or complex forest ecosystems such as the Amazon. Bioregions often are large locales, but they are small enough that the common good will be obvious

11. See "The Columbia River Watershed: Caring for Creation and the Common Good. An International Pastoral Letter by the Catholic Bishops of the Watershed Region."

12. See Anthony M. Pilla, "What the Church Brings the City: The Need for Community," *Origins* 30:15 (February 15, 2000), 237–240.

13. Another notable environmental project organized around the common good was the series of conversations organized in the Diocese of Houma-Thibodeaux, Louisiana, on the loss of arable land and productive marshes and estuaries due to the incursion of salt water. Subsidence and salinization of farm fields and the deterioration of marsh habitat, the natural hatchery for the shrimp, resulted from oil drilling in the same area. The diocese, led by Rob Gorman, then the social action director for the diocese, brought together various stakeholders—farmers, watermen, oilmen, businesspeople—to discuss the problems and the solutions they might advance in common. It was a fine example of the Church functioning as a convener of otherwise conflicted political interests (or "a community of moral discourse") in pursuit of the common good.

to most people in the region because of the felt immediacy of the issues. Likewise, for reasons of proximity, civic responsibility toward the environment can be more easily engaged in identifiable bioregions. That, at least, is the thesis of former Missoula, Montana, mayor, Daniel Kemmis in his book *Community and the Politics of Place.*[14] Because Montanans knew and loved their mountains, rivers, high plains, and ranch land, Kemmis argued, they understood what was being lost to exploitation by extractive industries owned by outside interests, and so should naturally have been ready to mobilize to protect their native land.

Bioregionalism illustrates the common good both as it applies to shared goods, in Kemmis' case natural beauty and natural resources of Montana, and to exercising civic and political responsibility for safeguarding those very goods. Bioregionalism is patriotism in the root sense of commitment to one's natural homeland. Bioregionalism, however, is restricted to localized natural systems. Today climate change raises the demands of the common good to a global level. Originally, the common good referred to the shared welfare of the citizens of ancient Greek city-states and of late medieval Italian communes and their immediate hinterlands. In modern times, it referred to the shared welfare of modern nation-states.[15] But in 1963, in a boldly prophetic move, Pope John XXIII, in his encyclical letter Peace On Earth *(Pacem in Terris)*, extended the concept to a world scale. "The universal common good," as he proposed it, consisted of those problems, like nuclear proliferation and disarmament, that neither single nations nor bilateral and multilateral treaties were capable of resolving, and for which transnational institutions might be required.[16] "The ecological crisis," as Pope John Paul II called it in his 1990 World Day of Peace Message "Peace With God the Creator, Peace with All Creation," has

14. Daniel Kemmis, *Community and the Politics of Place* (Norman, OK: University of Oklahoma Press, 1990).

15. For a full history and review of contemporary usage of the principle of the common good, see *Dictionary of Catholic Social Thought,* 192–197. Also, Drew Christiansen, S. J., "The Common Good and the Politics of Self-Interest: A Catholic Contribution to the Practice of Citizenship" in Donald Gelpi, ed., *Beyond Individualism: Toward a Retrieval of Moral Discourse in America* (Notre Dame, IN: University of Notre Dame Press, 1989).

16. See Pope John XXIII, *Pacem in Terris* "Peace on Earth" in *Catholic Social Thought,* nos. 130–145. Also, see Drew Christiansen, S. J., "Commentary on *Pacem in Terris* (Peace on Earth)" in Kenneth R. Himes, O.F.M., Lisa Sowle Cahill, Charles E. Curran, David Hollenbach, and Thomas A. Shannon, eds., *Modern Catholic Social Teaching: Commentaries and Interpretations* (Washington, DC: Georgetown University Press, 2005), 231–233.

particularly required responses governed by the common good for which new forms of global cooperation and governance are needed.[17] Satisfying moral demands entails a duty to establish the institutions to realize those ends. The Law of the Sea, the Montreal Protocol, and the Kyoto Protocol, as imperfect as they may be, represent institutions established to meet such planetary needs.

No environmental issue has shown as clearly as global warming the relevance of the principle of the universal common good. Here is a problem with countless sources across time and space, whose impact can be felt on every continent, that will affect this and future generations. For this reason, the U.S. bishops in "Renewing the Earth" spoke of the world's ecology as "the planetary common good."[18] The phrase connotes not just the notion that the universal common good is a transnational reality, but also that the specific good that is the focus of our concern is *the planet as a natural system.* Pope John Paul II caught the sense of the term in On Social Concern:

> *[O]ne cannot use with impunity different categories of being, whether living or inanimate—animals, plants, the natural elements—simply as one wishes, according to one's economic needs. On the contrary, one must take into account the nature of each being and of its mutual connections in an ordered system, which is precisely the "cosmos."*[19]

As a global commons, therefore, the atmosphere, atmospheric pollution, and the climate systems dependent on them are in an exceptional way matters of the planetary common good toward which "individuals, peoples, states and the international community," as Pope John Paul II noted, "bear duties and obligations."[20]

---

17. Pope John Paul II, "The Ecological Crisis: A Common Responsibility" in *"And God Saw It Was Good,"* nos. 9–10, 15, and *Centesimus Annus* "On The Hundredth Anniversary of *Rerum Novarum* in *Catholic Social Thought,* no. 40.

To take as an example the nuclear proliferation issue that was a concern to Pope John, the International Atomic Energy Agency, however imperfect, would represent the kind of transnational institution needed to realize the universal common good above and beyond what could be achieved by treaties alone.

18. "Renewing the Earth," 232–233.

19. *Sollicitudo Rei Socialis,* 34.

20. "Ecological Crisis," 15.

II. Social Justice and the Right to Development

> *And God is able to provide you with every blessing in abundance, so that by always having enough of everything, you may share abundantly in every good work* (II Corinthians 9:8).

Catholic involvement in the environmental movement has been complicated by two allied principles of Catholic social teaching: the right to development and the option for the poor.[21] In the past, some First-World environmentalists have been critical of promoting development, because it adds to exploitation of natural resources, pollution, urban sprawl, and global warming. So-called deep ecologists would reduce the world's human population and its standard of living so that all species might flourish in their needed habitat. Others simply fear that technological advancement by the global majority will stress the Earth beyond its carrying capacity. For that reason, they are likewise skeptical of the option for the poor.

For these critics, giving preference to the poor in the design of public policy may seem like a permissible indulgence, until it becomes clear in a world of limits, that "the haves" may have to bear a contraction of growth for the sake of "the have-nots," and even more, some sacrifices may be required of them in the name of equitable and sustainable development. But Catholic social teaching insists that those who are advantaged need to be ready to sacrifice their privileges so that those who are seriously disadvantaged may also enjoy their basic rights, or as I have written elsewhere, a life "with dignity and decency."[22] In On the Hundredth Anniversary of *Rerum Novarum* (*Centesimus Annus*, 1991) as he pleaded for "a worldwide effort to promote development," for example, Pope John Paul II made it clear that such an effort would involve "sacrificing the positions of income and of power enjoyed by

---

21. See "Renewing the Earth," 235–236. Also, see Drew Christiansen, S. J. "Learn a Lesson From the Flowers: Catholic Social Teaching and Global Stewardship" in Maura A. Ryan and Todd David Whitmore, eds., *The Challenge of Global Stewardship: Roman Catholic Responses* (Notre Dame, IN: Notre Dame University Press, 1997), 19–37. One controversial issue I do not discuss in this chapter but do treat in "Learn a Lesson From the Flowers" is the relation of population to development; see 32–33.

22. See Drew Christiansen, S. J., "Basic Needs: Criterion for the Legitimacy of Development" in Alfred Hennelly, S.J., and John Langan, S.J., eds., *Human Rights in the Americas: The Struggle for Consensus* (Washington, DC: Georgetown University Press, 1982), 244–288; on "dignity and decency," 259–262.

the more developed economies."[23] From an economic point of view, I understand, it may be objected that growth is necessary so that others may share in an improved quality of life. Economies cannot grow unless there are markets for their products. While I have made the case that sacrifices are and will be necessary in this global transition to equitable development in a sustainable environment, much of what may be described as "sacrifice" may be more appropriately described from an economic point of view as adjustments in economic policy. A carbon tax, repudiated when the Clinton-Gore team raised the possibility of a BTU tax in 1992, is now viewed, even by some in the energy and automobile sectors, as a rational economic policy.[24] The standards of economic rationality have changed. Many business people are today willing to consider expenditures in the interest of a sustainable global future a reasonable price for doing business. In 1992 they would have regarded these as sacrifices of expected income.

The deep ecologists aside, objections to the sacrifice of privilege demonstrate a sense of entitlement when it comes to using the Earth's resources. Climate change brings this problem to the fore: Many people simply can't imagine two and a half billion Chinese and Indians living at levels comparable to what the West enjoys today. Even more, they cannot imagine modifying our material lifestyle or political power to make way for an equitable and sustainable future for the planet. Objections in the 1990s to the Kyoto Protocols on the grounds that for the time being they did not set binding targets for carbon emissions for India and China are a prime instance of this sort of bias. Today it has become clear those giants must exercise responsibility in the future, and they need to be drawn into the next stage of the international effort to reduce greenhouse gases. It is encouraging to note that the so-called Plus 5 group (India and China, along with Brazil, Mexico, and South Africa) of the G8+5 signed a compact at the time of the G8 this month, agreeing in general terms to cut emissions as part of the new treaty that will replace the Kyoto Protocol

23. *Centesimus Annus*, 52.

24. On current business attitudes toward the carbon tax, see "Cleaning Up" (Leaders), 13 and "Everybody's Green Now," 13, *The Economist* (June 2, 2007), and in the same issue, Special Report, 3–4, 6. *The Economist* editorial (Leader), p. 6, actually backs a carbon tax as more helpful to business than a so-called cap and trade system. Critics explain, however, that while a carbon tax provides a more predictable economic environment, its environmental impact is less predictable than a cap and trade system.

in 2012. But the historical and actual burden of implementation of the protocols, at the time of the drafting and still today, lay with the West, and particularly the United States. The failure of Congress to ratify the Kyoto Protocols and then President Bush's withdrawal of the U.S. signature from the treaty were symptoms both of prejudice against the world's poor and of a profound reluctance to make the adjustments, adaptations, and sacrifices needed to avoid catastrophic global warming and consequent climate change. The sense of solidarity needed to act in the planetary common good was simply lacking. President Bush's agreement last week with the other G8 leaders to set a mandatory target of a 50-percent cut in emissions by 2050 marks a much-needed correction in U.S. policy. The hard part will be setting and implementing the policies, including mandatory limits on emissions, to effect that goal.

In Catholic social teaching, the right to property rests on what is called "the universal purpose of created things," that is, insofar as the goods of creation are available for human use, they are intended for the use of all.[25] The Creator provides them so that we all may flourish, and, accordingly, they should be available for the livelihood of all before being appropriated for anyone's private enrichment. Patristic theology spoke about "sufficiency" and "sharing" or "common use," that is, the Earth's resources are available for the welfare of all, and only when everyone's basic needs are met may the surplus be appropriated for private enjoyment. This teaching was renewed by the Second Vatican Council, and it lies at the heart of the teaching on the right to development by Paul VI and John Paul II.[26] All human beings, according to this teaching, have the right to the means to their own flourishing.[27]

Because of this right to development, Catholic social teaching has been especially concerned with distributive justice. Indeed much of Catholic teaching on economics deals with questions of distribution in the process of economic development and of the righting of

---

25. On the common purpose of created things, see *Gaudium et Spes*, 69. Also, Compendium of Social Doctrine, 329.
26. On the right to development, see Compendium of Social Doctrine, 446.
27. On the connection between economic development and personal flourishing, see Pope John XXIII, On Christianity and Social Progress *(Mater et Magistra)*, 65; also Pope Paul VI The Development of Peoples *(Populorum Progressio)*, 15–16, and Pope John Paul II, On Social Concern *(Sollicitudo Rei Socialis)*, 33.

inequalities in existing patterns of development.[28] Even John Paul's *Centesimus Annus*, best known for its defense of capitalism, especially in Eastern Europe, advocated "a concerted worldwide effort for promoting development." The body of social teaching is concerned with inequalities in levels of development. Indeed, in On the Development of Peoples *(Populorum Progressio)*, Pope Paul VI described the elaboration of institutions to rectify global inequalities in trade arrangements as "social justice."[29] He also identified the duty to sacrifice for the sake of equitable development.

> *Is [the rich man, that is, a member of an affluent society] prepared to support out of his own pocket works and understandings organized in favor of the destitute? Is he ready to pay higher taxes?...Is he ready to pay a higher price for imported goods?... Or to leave his country, if necessary and if he is young, in order to assist in [the] development of the young nations?*[30]

Catholic social teaching has insisted that environmental stewardship consists of equitable and sustainable development, and, in the intervening years, that has become at least the rhetorical goal of most of the industrial country governments.[31] *Sustainable development* refers to the management of environmental conditions such that the needs of this and future generations can be provided.[32] Stewardship involves serving as trustees for generations to come.

III. The Option for the Poor

> *"Then they also will answer, 'Lord, when was it that we saw you hungry or thirsty or a stranger or naked or sick or in prison, and did not take care of you?' Then he will answer them, 'Truly I tell*

---

28. See Drew Christiansen, S.J., "On Relative Equality: Catholic Egalitarianism After Vatican II," *Theological Studies* 45 (1984): 651–75.
29. *Populorum Progressio*, 56–75.
30. *Populorum Progressio*, 47.
31. *Centesimus Annus*, 52.
32. The term *sustainable development* was first used by the Brundtland Commission (formally the World Commission on Environment and Development) in its report *Our Common Future* (Oxford: Oxford University Press, 1987). Also, see Pope John Paul II, "Ecological Crisis," 6 and *Sollicitudo*, 33–34. Number 34 may be the most systematic statement of Catholic environmentalism to be found in official teaching.

> *you, just as you did not do it to one of the least of these, you did not do it to me'*" (Matthew 25:44–45).

In advance of the G8 meeting in Heiligendamm, Germany, Pope Benedict XVI urged the world leaders gathered there to give special consideration to the poor.[33] Similarly, presidents of the episcopal conferences of the G8 countries wrote their leaders asking them to make good on their pledges to the world's poor, especially in Africa. They wrote, "[W]e have a special concern for the poor. As a result of where they live and their limited access to resources, the poor will experience most directly the harmful effects of climate change and the burdens of any measures to address it, including potential escalating energy costs, worker displacement and health problems."[34] At the same time, the members of the National Religious Partnership for the Environment, including the USCCB, testified to Congress about the need to protect poor, vulnerable nations as the international community works to reverse global warming and to protect against and ameliorate the ill effects of climate change.[35] John L. Carr, speaking for the United States Catholic Conference, said "We should look at climate change from the 'bottom up' for how it touches the poor and vulnerable."[36] After a decade and a half, the priority of the poor continues to be a hallmark of the official Catholic approach to global climate change and

---

33. See Pope Benedict XVI, Letter to Chancellor Angela Merkel, May 31, 2007. Earlier the Pontifical Council for Justice and Peace had held a major conference on ethical dimensions of global climate change. See Pontifical Council for Justice and Peace, Study Seminar on Climate Change and Development, April 26–27, 2007 at www.justpax.it/eng/home_eng.html. For a comprehensive view of the Vatican's current international environmental policy by a leading diplomat, see Archbishop Celestino Migliore, "Catholic Faith Tradition of Stewardship" at www.ncrlc.com/Apostolic_Nuncio.html.
34. See USCCB Office of Media Relations, "Presidents of Seven Catholic Bishops Conferences Urge Group of 8 Countries to Take Bold Action on Urgent Global Problems," www.usccb.org/comm/archives/2007/07-094.shtml. The text of the communique is appended to this press release.
35. USCCB, Department of Social Development and World Peace, Letters of Bishop Thomas Wenski to the Hon. Jeff Bingaman, February 7, 2007, and to Hon. Barbara Boxer, June 7, 2007.
36. John L. Carr, "Written Testimony: Religious and Moral Dimensions of Global Climate Change," Committee on Environment and Public Works, United States Senate, June 7, 2007. I should also note that the Catholic Coalition on Climate Change, an outgrowth of the USCCB Environmental Justice Program, sponsored workshops in Florida, Ohio, and Alaska this spring and is receiving applications to support similar work across the country.

of ecumenical and interreligious participation in the environmental debate through the National Religious Partnership.

The Church's advocacy for the poor is rooted in its biblical witness. The common good and the right to development, though they also have biblical warrants, are usually formulated in philosophical language. Aid and defense of the poor, however, have immediate resonance in the Christian imagination: "Blessed are the poor"; "...Just as you did it to one of the least of these..."; "Which...was a neighbor to the man who fell into the hands of the robbers?" Drawing from liberation theology, in On Social Concern Pope John Paul II spoke of the Church's *option* or *love of preference* for the poor," usually termed "the preferential option for the poor."[37] He made it clear in the succeeding passages that the preferential option for the poor should be the center point in the design of international policy. In official Catholic social teaching it remains so, even as the question of development has grown more complex due to the need to deal simultaneously with environmental issues.

In formulating global environmental policy, the pressing question, especially for American policymakers, has been "Are there weighted or differential responsibilities for rich and poor justified in a global compact for sustainable development?" The answer to this question prompts even more queries: Should some allowance be made for developing nations, especially the so-called giants, in view of the underdevelopment of the majority of their population? Do developed nations have obligations, not in charity, but in justice, to help poor nations even as they pay the price for their own pollution? On these issues, Catholic social teaching is unequivocal. Developed economics have responsibilities to promote sustainable development in the Two-Thirds World, and this applies even in the constricted circumstances created by global warming and the adjustments it requires in patterns of postindustrial development.

Pope John Paul II made clear in his 1990 World Day of Peace message that sharing the Earth's resources in the interest of sustainable

37. *Sollicitudo*, 42–43. "A Preferential Option for the Poor" was the title of the concluding document of the 1979 Puebla meeting of the Council of Episcopal Conferences of Latin America (CELAM). For further background and analysis, see "Poor, Preferential Option For," in Judith A. Dwyer and Elizabeth L. Montgomery, eds., *Dictionary of Catholic Social Thought* (Collegeville, MN: Liturgical Press, 1994), 755–759.

development must be sustained within the circumscribed environmental limits of today's world. He wrote:

> *The newly industrialized States cannot, for example, be asked to apply restrictive environmental standards in their emerging industries unless the industrialized States first apply them within their own boundaries. At the same time, countries in the process of industrialization are not morally free to repeat the errors made in the past by others, and recklessly continue to damage the environment.*[38]

There is a presumption, therefore, that developed nations have greater responsibilities to making global collaboration work. The duties are properly differential. Developed nations, because of their historic exploitation of resources, their current levels of pollution, and their material advantages, have primary responsibility to build a global system for sustainable development that includes reducing "greenhouse gases."

Developing countries, especially those in a "takeoff" mode, also have responsibilities of restraint, but the burden, in the first instance, is with developed countries. In an unequal world, disparate schedules and special allowances, as found in the Kyoto Protocols, Rio, and the other relevant international agreements are in principle morally, not just politically, necessary.

Pope John Paul II captured this perspective on First-World responsibilities with appeals to the story of Lazarus and the Rich Man. In Development of Peoples *(Populorum Progressio)*, with a remarkable turn of phrase, Pope Paul VI reversed the parable, writing of building a world "where [everyone]...can live truly human lives...where the poor man Lazarus can sit down with the rich man at the same table."[39] Echoing that theological reversal, Pope John Paul wrote in On Social Concern that in solidarity we "see the 'other'..."as our 'neighbor,' a 'helper' (see Genesis 2:18–20), to be made a sharer, on a par with ourselves, in the banquet of life to which all are equally invited by God."[40] The challenge of sustainable development, therefore, is not just to preserve the Earth as we know it, but to do so in a way that favors the

---

38. "Ecological Crisis," 10.
39. *Populorum Progressio*, 47.
40. *Sollictudo*, 39.

integral development of the world's poor. The image of Lazarus and the Rich Man makes clear, however, that in meeting this challenge the heaviest obligation falls on the rich.

In addressing the issue of sustainable development, Pope John Paul II alternately chided developed countries for their failures and encouraged them to reach still higher. The story of Lazarus and the Rich Man stands over his appeals like a great medieval altarpiece. The original Lukan story, a tragic parable of condemnation for indifference to the poor, stands behind the pope's warnings. The imaginative reversal of the parable proposed by Pope Paul VI—the vision of Lazarus and the Rich Man sitting down to table together—is a message of positive encouragement. It is a parable Pope John Paul II pointedly addressed to U.S. audiences during his visits here. "Do you not think," he once asked, "that this parable applies to you?"

Of First-World responsibilities toward the world's poor, Pope John Paul II wrote, "If a nation were to succumb more or less deliberately to the temptation to close in upon itself and failed to meet the responsibilities following from its superior position in the community of nations, it *would fall seriously short* of its clear ethical duty"[41] (emphasis added). The Church's prophetic message is clear. The fate of the planet and of the human family, so tightly intertwined, depends, in large part, on a wholesale conversion of the American people and, in Pope John Paul II's words, the birth of "a new religious awareness" of our responsibilities to life on Earth leading to a transformation of the American role in the world. That is the Church's challenge to America and a very specific challenge for American Catholics.

---

41. *Sollicitudo*, 23.

Panel Discussion

Moderator: Richard W. Miller II

Panel: Rev. Michael Himes
David O'Brien
Kristin Heyer
Rev. Kenneth Himes, O.F.M.
Lisa Sowle Cahill
Rev. Drew Christiansen, S.J.

Richard Miller: One of the general questions that was asked is one that I can answer. Several people asked, "Where do you get the American Bishops Guidelines, 'Faithful Citizenship'?" You can go to the Internet and do a search, USCCB (United States Catholic Conference of Bishops), "Faithful Citizenship," and the document is right there. There's a whole Web site for that (http://www.usccb.org/faithfulcitizenship/).

This question is for the entire panel. A theme running through this and some other questions was, "Why don't we know more about 'Faithful Citizenship'? Why isn't it more public? How do we, the faithful, urge or influence the bishops to support their own document?"

Michael Himes: Building on what you said, Rich, I think one of the reasons is because the document is so balanced, it's so nuanced. And it's very hard to get the press interested in a very nuanced, balanced document. We so often hear that phrase of "politics or government by sound bite." And of course sound bites only work if you are going take a position that you can say in two or three sentences and get it on the evening news. Well, the very essence of what the bishops do in "Faithful Citizenship" is not sound bites.

The moment you start saying there are fifty issues and they interlock and you cannot eliminate any one of them or emphasize one of them at the expense of others, you've eliminated the possibility of a sound bite; the problem is the media just don't know how to deal with that. They aren't good at reporting that kind of that thing. It's precisely the nuance that is the glory of the document and the problem of getting it explained, getting it noted.

Drew Christiansen: Just to say one thing to explain the bishops' conference. The conference really doesn't have any capacity for implementation. Really they serve the bishops and their local diocese; it's up to the local bishops to decide the degree to which they will use the materials that are produced by the conference. The Social Development of World Peace Office does much work on behalf of their committees in the conference, lobbying before Congress, carrying out educational programs, but they don't really have a capacity to call a press conference or to develop a media strategy. That's not their job. So you can look at some dioceses during 2004. Some areas—the state of Michigan, for example—the Michigan State Catholic Conference did a terrific job with "Faithful Citizenship" and with a whole process of making materials available to the Detroit media, trying to work the media in the Michigan area, getting material to parishes to use precisely to try to head off other groups like the Catholic Answers text. So it's really up to each diocese to decide how to use these materials. And I should say schools and religious orders as well.

Richard Miller: This question is for Father Michael Himes: "If conscience is formed by community, what happened when the community is messed up?"

Michael Himes:: You get messed-up consciences. Quite honestly. I'll give you the obvious and extreme example of this, which is Germany and the Third Reich. If you are successfully acculturated, introduced into, if you were a successful participant in Germany in the '30s, imagine what your view of the world has to be. Or what it is to be a human being, or who counts as human beings, how you relate to other human beings, and precisely everything around you. Everyone around you reinforces that, "Yes, that's exactly right, you're doing the right thing; the way you think, the way you're treating those people is precisely the right way you are to act." And so you end up having people, you know, the familiar picture of the wonderfully cultivated, the marvelously cultured person, who is also a guard at an extermination camp. How do you put those two things together? You have a thoroughly distorted conscience. But that thoroughly distorted conscience isn't simply the pathology of that individual, it's the product of a whole society that has forced it and produced that individual. That's why, as I tried to suggest this morning, the individual has to work to change the community, the community is also changing the individual. Unbalance that in either direction and it causes immense problems. It really requires something quite astonishing to break through that kind of situation.

Now it does happen. Witness earlier today, as a matter of fact. David was mentioning to me a film that I have not seen yet—I intend to—but many of you may have. A film called *Amazing Grace,* about the abolition of the slave trade in England and Wilberforce's role in that abolition. How do you explain William Wilberforce? How do you explain a Martin Luther King? How do you explain a Gandhi? How do you explain a Nelson Mandela? How do you explain a Dorothy Day? How do you explain someone whose conscience is so rich, so nuanced, so inclusive in a society that seems to militate against that?

One thing that should be said about grace, certainly in a Catholic context, is that every now and again the grace of God surprises you. It breaks through, and there is no accounting for this, other than this is grace at work in people's lives. So that does, thank God, happen. It is also a good, old Catholic principle that you "don't bank on grace." Don't presume it. Grace always comes as an undeserved gift. The moment you start banking on it you violate it, but grace has got to be taken into account on these issues.

Richard Miller: There were a few questions for the entire panel regarding the controversy about the use of Communion as punishment in the last election. One of the questions is, "Where do the bishops get the right to refuse Communion to people who are pro-choice or politicians who are pro-choice platform, and so on?"

Lisa Cahill: I'll say something about it, but David, would you have anything to say about it historically or canonically, even? I guess the one thing I'll say—but this is not probably the most fundamental thing that should be said—is there is a legitimate concern about whether it's ever appropriate publicly to exclude certain people from the community who have transgressed its norms in some outrageous way. That's controversial. I'm not saying which side we should come down on, but another example that is sometimes given is the excommunication in Latin America—like in Pinochet's Chile—of people who were known torturers or who sought to torture victims of the repressive state. And so they were excluded, and that was a way that the Church took a stand with the poor and the victimized. So it's not so easy as to just say, "We should never rule anyone out."

Okay, but then the next issue is why this? Why on abortion? And I would say two things. First, it was applied very inconsistently on one issue, not on the panorama of issues that should have been considered. And only abortion was targeted as an issue, whereas there are all these other fifty issues, some of very significant importance. And then, even abortion was targeted in an extremely simplistic way, because it was done without looking at whether someone was really working to reduce abortion. The issue was only identified in terms of whether someone was willing to attack *Roe v. Wade*. If they weren't in favor of recriminalizing abortion, they were excommunicated. And that was without any regard to the evidence that Rich, for example, showed this morning about how the legality and the illegality of abortion is not, in fact, what determines whether abortion is used. In fact, in 1967, as he said, there were more abortions than in 1997. So that's not really the issue. So how committed are we to really reducing the causes of abortion? What would that take? What kind of sacrifice would that require? And who are the bishops willing to confront on that, and who are they not? I think the Republican Party—and I'm from Massachusetts, I am obviously a Democrat—is often very, very out there with its anti-abortion, pro-life rhetoric. But it's not out there in terms of providing support to the middle class, the working class, and the poor that would actually help prevent abortions. There also is the issue of education and availability of contraception that Rich raised. So it's not that excommunication is necessarily always wrong; it's the way it was *targeted* and done in this case, but that's not an answer on the basis of canon law or history.

Drew Christiansen: Let me add that the bishops' way of handling this is to try to work together, to have an answer. In those situations, people who are willing to break ranks and speak on their own have an advantage in getting press attention. And bishops then put it into process. McCarrick and his committee got something they wanted, they went to Rome, where Ratzinger signed off on it. In fact, the story is really that when some people in his office tried to spin it a different way, he had the document rewritten to fit what the American bishops as a whole wanted, and McCarrick came back and reported that. Then the really politically adept infighters got hold of it, and they attacked McCarrick with full-page ads and so on and put him out on his own. It's a shame that other bishops were reluctant to come out and speak. I think it's probably good that they have learned a certain reluctance about being too forward about these issues. But I think a lot has to do with the willingness of some who are tough fighters by nature to break the rules to make their point. Those who play by the rules get caught and can't respond in a sufficiently strong way.

Richard Miller: This question is for Dr. O'Brien: "If you had five minutes and were speaking to a group with a limited vocabulary, what would be your simplified key message for successfully striving for the goals set by the bishops' 'Faithful Citizenship'?"

David O'Brien: I've been focusing, and I certainly focused in my talk today, on the question of why there wasn't more organized support among Catholics, especially Catholic professionals and semiprofessionals, people who work for the Church, especially in ministries that have a stake in "Faithful Citizenship," as well as those who are teachers and professors and semiprofessionals in the Church. And why the political dynamic within the Church now is such that much of the game seems it is being won by the conservatives and it's not challenged. The question for that issue would be to find out what one could about the preparation of the current document. There's been almost no outside organization from the center and left of the spectrum around either the reorganization of the conference, which is a whole question to get into, or the letter.

If you wanted to ask the question, "How would you take 'Faithful Citizenship' as a citizen and implement it?", well, that's a little different. Remember, we're not advocating for a kind of left-wing Democratic Party document. We're advocating for Catholic social teaching being known, the formation of conscience. Do what the bishops say in the letter to help the community form its conscience on the occasion of a national election. As I've said, there are dioceses in the country—Cleveland a few years ago, until recently, Michigan—that have done an excellent job of using that text in parishes, in regional bodies, organizing public forums, having a lot of commentary in the local diocesan newspaper, getting clips on the election or specific issues to be featured in parish bulletins. Materials are available to help educate the public and to raise those questions. If you have a particular issue that you really want to raise in the election and people aren't really paying attention, there are techniques to reach the media and get attention for your question. So, in each case, whether it's in the Church or outside the Church, the answer is the old adage: organize. You have to organize; we can't do these things alone, but you have to find people of similar interest and organize to try to have an impact on the process. Is this what people are asking for?

Richard Miller: Yes, and then I'll follow that up, and this can go to the whole panel. Do you have any suggestions about how grassroots people may come to understand and then act on the principles of the common good? Parish groups, local civic groups, youth groups, maybe even congregations. This is the issue: how do you organize?

Kristin Heyer: In terms of community organizing, a recent, enormously helpful resource from the Catholic Campaign for Human Development (CCHD) is titled "Credible Signs of Christ Alive." It integrates the theoretical framework many of us have presented today—the backdrop of Catholic social teaching in conversation—with profiles of different community organizing projects that CCHD has sponsored and funded. These include people organizing for affordable housing in Camden, people working for a living wage ordinance in Baltimore, the Delmarva Poultry Justice Alliance, and people at my home parish in Los Angeles doing community organizing in east LA for community safety. Even if you're not talking about community organizing, each of these other constituencies is nice because it really marries the theory and practice in an accessible way with questions for discussion, reflection tools, kind of excerpts—not quite sound bites—digestible insights from these encyclicals rather than perhaps long, dry quotations. So I would suggest that resource.

Richard Miller: Will you repeat the resource for people?

Kristin Heyer: The source is *Credible Signs of Christ Alive: Case Studies for the Catholic Campaign for Human Development* (Rowman & Littlefield Publishers, 2003). The author is listed as John P. Hogan.

Richard Miller: The common good has been a common theme, so several questions have emerged. Kristin dealt with that explicitly, but all of you have been drawing on that. So this question is open to all of you: "How can the common good be expressed given a pluralistic society with many different ways of naming the good?" Let me also add this to your burden: "Is the common good based on a set of values that transcend a particular religious tradition, and if so, on, or by what authority?"

Kristin Heyer: David Hollenbach—a colleague of most of these folks whom I should thank for not being able to be here today because I get to be here—in his book on the common good talks about a phrase I didn't use, called *dialogical universalism,* which may confuse this question when I want to clarify it, but I think it's really helpful in terms of this idea. I did mention his intellectual solidarity, different groups engaging one another on these questions of fundamental meaning, what makes the good life, in conversation with one another.

The reason I mention virtues like humility or approaches like persuasion is this idea, back to Michael's first lecture, that no one of us is pinning down the common good, the transcendent. So any kind of human approximation is always relativized. And it really should be, in conversation with other communities about the nature of the good, and in particular, the nature of the shared good. I think Hollenbach grounds that nicely in both philosophy and theology, certainly in kind of a Vatican II legacy of taking the signs of the times seriously in conversation with our own Catholic tradition, and then in conversation, as I mentioned, with sciences and other religions.

Kenneth Himes: One of the "standard formulas" that many people in political life use is that while there's a diversity to happiness, there's usually unity to misery. There is a lot of truth in that. Going back to Michael's earlier question, if you ask people "What do you really love?" As Michael said, you get a great range of views about what people really love, and sometimes people love inordinately the things that are of very limited value. So you can get skewed approaches to things. It's fairly easy, actually, to get some unity around the things that we fear or that we worry about. Nobody's really going to come out with a defense of hunger. No one's in support of wanton violence. Nobody cheers on disease.

The fact of the matter is, if you start with a universal claim, as Kristin was suggesting earlier with regard to human dignity, and as Michael had mentioned, the Catholic claim is we do this not because *you're* Catholic, we do this because *we're* Catholic. We care about human dignity, *anyone's* human dignity. You can get a fair amount of accord around, "What are the serious threats to human dignity? What are those things that genuinely do threaten and undermine human flourishing?" Therefore, I think the idea that in a pluralistic society, and an even more pluralistic world, that the task of forging alliances and building regimes that gather around and are willing to combat and fight for certain goods is a mistaken approach. If you are focusing on trying to make people all agree on how we define the lifestyle we want to choose, that becomes nearly impossible. But if you're trying to build support for coalitions of people that will work against certain things that deeply threaten human well-being and human dignity, it's not that difficult a project to try to build consensus.

Drew Christiansen: Let me return to the question of convening; this relates to what Kristin had to say about dialogue. I mentioned the work that Rob Gorman did in Thibodaux: bringing together people on various sides of the loss of the wetlands in southern Louisiana. Let me give two other examples. One is an effort that Bishop John Cummins in Oakland carried out after the '83 pastoral letter on peace with scientists from the Lawrence Livermore National Laboratory and the critics in the Oakland diocese. On the one hand, the pastoral letter created a great deal of interest on the part of the critics in being able to finger the people of Lawrence Livermore, which is one of the national laboratories that designs, produces, and tests weapons. It created a great deal of anxiety among Catholics there about their jobs and by others whether they were doing the right thing. For several years, Cummins convened meetings to bring the scientists together with their critics and other experts in international affairs and so on to discuss the issues. As a result of changing times, as much as anything else, Lawrence Livermore said for a long time, until this administration, that the bishop changed the direction it was going. I also know that in some cases, people chose to change their careers so they went into testing and verification and issues like that, rather than in weapons design because of that kind of discussion. Another is the Pew Center on Global Climate Change, which is located in Virginia. They brought together scientists with environmentalists and other social activists, including people from the churches and businesspeople, to develop an alliance on climate change. They eventually developed a list of corporations that were willing to go along and sign with their principles until even some of their major critics and opponents began to join them in the community. So convening and dialogue, when you can bring together different groups, is very important. I think it's a particularly important function for the Church as a community where various people from different places come together. Where my grandfather and social life comes from, Jim Gustafson talked about the Church as a community of moral discourse. I think it is that, and we can take advantage of it.

Lisa Cahill: Let me just say that I really agree with both these points. First, it's not difficult to determine what are basic human goods, that most cultures and people want the same basic things. Second, the way you agree on concrete arrangements is through dialogue, not from some authority above handing it down, as the question suggested. I want to add a third point, too. And this is the thing that's most difficult to agree on and that is a real problem for morality. It is not, "What are the minimum basic goods?" Rather it is, "Who's entitled to access?" So it's the issue of equality, or human rights in a modern terminology, the human dignity, universal human dignity. In modern Catholic social teaching and in premodern thought and in many societies in the world today that is not taken for granted.

If you refer to the classical sources, people were mentioning Aristotle this morning. "Oh, the *polis*, the good society!" And I kept thinking, "Yeah, except for the women and the slaves"—because it was taken for granted and still is—in most societies that some, us, we, an elite, me and my friends, my associates, we are entitled. But the hard case to make is that everyone is equally entitled. When you have a situation of conflict over limited resources, as Drew talked about with global climate change in the developing world, in China versus the United States, and everybody saying, "You first." "No, you first." It's because we want access to this global public good.

Everybody agrees, but no one agrees that everyone else has equal access or that they need to make sacrifices and we need to make sacrifices—all of us together. So it's the equality issue that is a modern Western conception, by and large. I mean, you can find roots of it in the New Testament and in Christian tradition, but it's not as easily universal as basic goods.

So, what are the basic goods? Who gets the basic goods? And who's going to have to sacrifice? Who gets the benefits and who bears the burdens? Those are the hard moral issues.

David O'Brien: It's equality but it's also democracy. It's what process do you set up, and do you really allow everybody to participate? You say you want everybody to be included. Well, how's the process going to work that really can include everybody in defining, "What is the common good?" That's a classic problem in American history; read the tenth essay by Madison in the *Federalist Papers*. Throughout our history we've had a very difficult time doing that except in wartime. War is the one time where we're able to mobilize everybody, at least in the good wars. And when President Roosevelt spoke of the New Deal, in the early New Deal he kept using the analogy of the First World War. Look what we accomplished when we got together in the First World War. We had to do that to overcome the Depression. John Kennedy used the phrase, "The war on poverty."

Ronald Reagan, in his remarkable inaugural address, had a kind of schizophrenic thing: on the one hand government is the problem, we have to leave things to the marketplace and domestic policy; on the other hand, government is the instrument of our national honor abroad. Therefore, we have to have as much military power as we need in the hands of the government to protect our national interest abroad. So, we have that bifurcated thing; in most of our social policy we have had compensatory policies, but not policies really framed around the public interest of the common good unless they touched on national defense.

We can see this, I think, in the very difficult problem of formulating a national health care plan, even though probably a majority of constituencies recognize the need for it. That is where I come back to my Americanism piece at the end of my discussion; I really do think we need to recover some kind of emotional sense of national solidarity. You mention Robert Bella. Twice Robert Bella spoke to Catholic groups and pleaded with Catholics to draw upon their tradition, which Kristin described so well as having that strong doctrine of the common good. Bella hoped that tradition was part of our experience, too, from our urban and ethnic neighborhoods where we had a sense of solidarity that we could bring to the American mix, a kind of sense of the common good in solidarity and interdependence that was necessary. I think he was disappointed that we weren't better at that.

Lately I have been talking a lot about moments in our history when people experience a sense of national solidarity: on hearing John Kennedy's inaugural address, how many people's lives were changed? They changed their lives because of his plea to people to ask not what their country can do for them but what they can do for their country. Martin Luther King's "I Have a Dream" speech" still will touch reservoirs of a sense of possibility and hope in people. Reaction to 9/11: I was obsessed myself with reading everything I could get my hands on about 9/11, but especially those profiles of individuals in *The New York Times* day after day after day. I can put together a talk with Jim Dwyer's reporting about how so many of us felt that enormous sense of solidarity with one another and kind of a sense of American pride. So it is a missing piece. It's amazing, I think.

John McGreevy, the chairman of the history department of Notre Dame, and I had a conversation one night. John argues that the great change in the second half of the twentieth century in the United States is the conservative move all across the board and in every phase of American life, and one aspect of it was a sense of decline in our sense of the common good, the public interest. Without a recovery of this, it is hard to see how we are going to be able to reinvigorate our politics. So it is a really big question with many pieces. Public interest and common good are not quite the same, but they all turn around some sense of solidarity, some sense that we really are invested in each other. This is something really worth working on.

Richard Miller: How do we deal with the dominance of economic issues in this country and capitalism with its roots in American life? So, how do you deal with the dominance of economic issues the Church is teaching and the dominance of economic issues in the present life and capitalism in American history? How do you deal with that in relation to the Church's teaching?

David O'Brien: That's a very large question, and I don't know quite how to deal with that. Many of us, of course, were around when the bishops were working on their pastoral letter in 1986 on the economy of human inventions and a number of things about that. They start out to talk about capitalism, which was actually the proposition that was voted on by the bishops for us to do a pastoral letter on capitalism. They got into that and it was so complex they couldn't get a handle on it. So they did a commentary on selected problems in the American economy. Following the process by which they wrote that letter—going back and reading the letter—is helpful.

Their process was precisely what we're talking about here. They drew upon the norms of common good and public interest and option for the poor. All of these offered a rich, complicated kind of commentary, and their answer to the systemic question was the section they called the "New

American Experiment." This was very modest. It wasn't anticapitalist; it was more that they were trying to draw upon their own experience. Many experienced community organizing and community development corporations that set a mood and a spirit of experiment, building private partnerships to bring about economic development areas of poverty and where there were needs for economic development.

As I said in my talk, one of the things I said at the time and I have really believed since is that it was a wonderful letter. I thought the "New American Experiment" section was a very venturesome thing for them: to actually say what a democratic political economy would look like. One component would be community organizing lots of ways for people to organize to get a place at the table. Another piece would be collaboration across these barriers to work on defined common community problems. But when they got to the pastoral section—the section on what we should *do*—over the course of three drafts, it got much weaker, I thought. It came down to a lot of prayer stuff and they got this anti-, this counter-cultural business about materialism and having the family as a haven. They increasingly shrank over the drafts the call to laypeople to see their work, their participation in the economy, as part of the web of their kind of lives for holiness and that the faith is tested for us in how we live our lives. They really reduced that concept. I thought that was a foundation to awaken a sense of lay vision, lay ministry, a kind of purposefulness of lay life around vocation and work that really didn't get included. So there was not a good implementation strategy (as I called it), though I think if you read the entire letter and paid particular attention to the section on the New American Experiment, you would find it a very rich beginning place for the discussion.

Michael Himes: If I may just include one other consideration here, I don't think there is anything wrong with capitalism in itself. Capitalism isn't a bad thing in itself. The problem with capitalism is too often it's presented as the *only* thing, and then it becomes a bad thing. I go back to my comment this morning about idolatry: the moment you start to think that the truth you perceive, which may indeed be true, is *the* truth, the only truth, the whole truth, and the truth that everybody else ought to perceive as the whole truth, you have a big problem.

Capitalism has worked very well for a great many people in certain circumstances. It has hurt other people in other circumstances, and it might not work in different circumstances in the places where it has worked under the initial circumstances. It is a way of organizing a society and an economy. The mistake is to absolutize it as the *only* way. Indeed in many ways—and I suppose this is true of almost any century, but in the twentieth century it's just so obvious—the twentieth century was an enormous battle in the Western world between pretended absolutes.

Communism has the true vision of the future. Read Marx and you will know exactly where the economy is ending up and how inevitably—I mean adjust the time table periodically—but *inevitably,* Comrades, we're all going to end up in a classless society because this is not *a* truth; this is *the* truth. Capitalism did exactly the same thing from the other side: Marxism is utterly wrong because *we* were utterly right. Communism was clearly flawed because we had the truth and the whole truth and there was no other truth. The mistake is setting up battling absolutes. The idea that capitalism is inevitably "the enemy" is a mistake. The idea that capitalism is inevitably your friend is a mistake.

Capitalism is one way of organizing society and human experience, and human history is infinitely more diverse, infinitely more complex, infinitely more confusing, than any system—political or economic—that attempts to reduce the experience to its own boundaries. So let's not ask how are we going to counter capitalism. How are we going to bring capitalism down to a becoming realism about its limitations? That is what's needed, not simply a rejection of capitalism as always and in every case a bad thing.

Drew Christiansen: Let me just add a note here. Ryan Lieber is a Protestant theologian who is famous for his analyses of power; he argued that the only way to restrain power is by countervailing power. He was saying that particularly for application to international affairs, but it applied to his earlier years, to what he thought about domestic affairs and his day back in the '20s and '30s, when labor was a source for controlling capitalism. It is hard to see how labor can be reinvigorated to be a significant curb on the excesses of capitalism today. Politics as another one, especially in the Great Depression, but again the American system has not been very good politically at curbing capitalism, especially when there's a major crisis like the Depression. But I think we need to look. If you want to attend to that, you need to look there. You need also to look to the education of business people and the media. The media has some tapes in its head that eventually become public agenda. The sexual revolution is certainly one of the things in their agenda for good or ill, but the environmental problem is another that they have put on the public agenda worldwide. Being able to influence the media may be one way to exercise countervailing power with respect to capitalism.

Richard Miller: This is a follow-up question: "Help me think through globalization through a Catholic lens." I told you when I invited you, it wouldn't be easy. This is for all of you. So there's no escape.

Kenneth Himes: Let me say something from my limited diplomatic experience. I was a delegate for the Vatican to the World Trade Organization (WTO) meeting in Seattle, the one that you thought failed because of the rioters in the street. But it failed because of the ham-fisted way in which the Clinton administration ran this meeting. It did not allow member nations to come together to meet in the committees that were supposed to knock out the policy. They had groups of the industrial nations, that is, the European Union, the United States, South Africa, and Australia perhaps, but they did not invite the Third-World countries that were supposedly equal members into those sessions. The beginning of globalization is to allow equal participation in those kinds of forums like the WTO. The WTO is not running because, like a lot of so-called free trade, it was really managed trade and is still managed in favor of the benefit of the leading nations.

The Vatican's position was to talk about the need for development and so on for leading nations. We walked the halls, and later when I talked about the arrogance of power there as a reason for resentment against the United States following 9/11, one of the negotiators for the United States came up and said, "You just don't understand the pressures from the clothing and textile manufacturers in South Carolina." Well, that's why we are not handling globalization very well. We did it in a very ham-fisted way and globalization is now not the kind of dynamic that it was five or six years ago. It is now kind of caught and spinning its wheels, it seems to me.

Richard Miller: This is for Father Himes., Oh, yes, there are two of you! Father Michael Himes.

Michael Himes: The good Himes.

Richard Miller: The good Himes. And then, Kristin, there will be questions for you on immigration, so it will tie these together. For Father Michael Himes: Your statement on human rights as broader than citizenship seems to have implications regarding the issue of immigration.

Michael Himes: Yes, you're right. It certainly does. It has implications for a whole slew of things. Immigration is certainly one of them. The one that I was thinking you might be thinking of when I said it is the treatment of prisoners at Guantanamo Bay, where we argue about whether they have the rights of citizens in access to a legal system, as if only American citizens have a right to a speedy trial, a just procedure, and open...to have advocacy, to have assistance in defending themselves, to know what they're accused of. Are those simply the rights of citizens, or are those the rights of human beings?

Now there is (and much has been written about this) a certain tension between the Declaration of Independence and the Constitution. The Constitution talks about the formation of a kind of compact among the states, for the good of the states: "In order to form a more perfect union." In order to bring about national well-being, that's why we are forming the Constitution. The Declaration of Independence is a much bigger document, much broader document than the Constitution. The Declaration of Independence says we are human beings and as human beings we possess certain rights. And it is becoming on us—there is an obligation on us—to give an account to the rest of humanity for our actions in rebelling against the English crown and Parliament. And that is because the rest of humanity has a right to ask us, "Why are you doing what you are doing?" It is all about human rights in the eighteenth century.

Jefferson would not have used the language of "human rights," but that is what he is talking about. The Constitution really reflects a somewhat different background than the Declaration itself. It seems to me if we are going to take the Declaration as a founding document along with the Constitution—and in many ways that was the whole of Abraham Lincoln's political agenda: to insist that the fundamental law of the land was not just the Constitution but the Constitution *and* the Declaration of Independence—then Guantanamo, it seems to me, becomes something we need to give an account of to the rest of the human race, and I think we will find it very awkward to try and give that account.

I think the same thing is true about the question of immigration, the question of who has...is there a limitation? Do nation-states trump the right of individuals to movement around the globe, to movement from one place to another, to movement a few miles from one side of the Rio Grande to a few miles to the other side of the Rio Grande? Is that trumped by the fact that there are national boundaries?

Are nation-states the only way in which we can imagine the human race being organized? They weren't before the seventeenth century the normal way people organized societies. The Middle Ages didn't know anything about nation-states. The Middle Ages were organized by feudalism, quite different from the nation-state. It is interesting that it may be after 400 years we are seeing the nation-states start to disappear. One wonders whether the Treaty of Maastricht that brings about the European Union, that if in Europe, where the nation-state began, the nation-state is now slowly disappearing, passing off the scene as something that has served its time in the course of human history and is now not a particularly good way to organize human communities. So I think, yes, it does raise great questions about immigration. It raises great questions about Guantanamo. It raises great questions about the use of torture for any purposes whatsoever. It raises lots and lots of questions, and I would point out that I am not raising those questions. Thomas Jefferson did!

Richard Miller: Kristin, here are some questions on immigration. The first one is: "What is the Church's position on illegal immigration?" This is the second question, "In terms of our nation's common good, undocumented immigrants are illegal immigrants. We are carrying their burden by paying for their education, health care, and child care needs. How do we tackle the issue for the common good?"

Kristin Heyer: Thank you. You know, my first couple of projects after graduate school I worked on religion and politics and some disagreements in Catholic social ethics. When I was finished, I thought my next project should be something less controversial since these were taxing…so now I have taken up undocumented immigration and social sin!

I realize these are controversial issues. I think the bishops' position, again very much rooted in universal human rights, human dignity, as well as the concept of the common good and a few others I mentioned, is that the reality at present is we have a broken system. I think people on many sides of the issue can agree with that. Our president has talked about people in the shadows; you know, we need to bring people out of the shadows. I know I mentioned five or so positions of the bishops. Maybe I could just elaborate on two.

First, they want to bring the realities of separated families and labor demands into better conformity with our system, with our laws. We have many families of mixed status here, mixed immigration status. We have these backlogs and the conversations in the last few weeks have started to talk about point systems—really treating people more as economic units than treating them in terms of their full humanity—so with the family such a central unit of society, that is a matter of concern.

Second, the labor demands. I think we have something like 5,000 H2A and H2B visas every year and the demand is something like 500,000 low-wage jobs, so there is a real mismatch. There wouldn't be such a strong magnet if people were not being employed in high numbers. Not only are they employed, but exploited—there are a lot of studies on day-labor abuses. So ways to find more safe, humane, legal pathways—whether through guest worker programs, pathways to legalization, and citizenship—seem to make sense to a lot of coalitions.

I recognize the tension here in terms of the national common good, maybe especially stresses on local services—the question mentioned child care and health care—I think one helpful thing about the bishops' Justice for Immigrants Web site is that it has a helpful link about myths on immigration. One myth about immigrants, "Obviously they pay no taxes," is kind of premised in this question. I think most studies show that there is somewhat of a net win for the U.S. economy when you consider sales tax, Medicare, and Social Security being paid in by undocumented immigrants. But certainly there is this tension with kind of a tax on local services that improvement to our federal system would help.

The other thing I want to say is that most studies show that many undocumented immigrants are competing mostly with other immigrants, not displacing native-born workers. But I think one thing that I do want to say in response. Cardinal Mahoney's pretty outspoken on this issue. He complains that there has been a kind of scapegoating of undocumented immigrants for many of our nation's ills, particularly the conflation of terrorism. This is understandable, but heightened security interests and securing the southwestern border and immigration are being connected in a way that the facts do not really bear out. We haven't caught any suspected terrorists crossing the southwestern border.

So it is important to bring up ways in which that is problematic according to Catholic social teaching. I think it relates more to the globalization questions that Drew was addressing. I think it is all a piece. You cannot look at free trade and fair trade without these patterns of migration. And until we move from an opportunistic interdependence with countries like Mexico and Central American countries, for instance, toward some type of globalization without marginalization and with an eye toward solidarity, we are not going to get to the root of these problems.

Richard Miller: This is for Ken Himes, and I'm sure the rest of you can help him on this one: "What do you think on Catholic principles about what we can do in Iraq with our very limited options?"

Kenneth Himes: I think obviously if there were an easy answer, we would have hit on it long before this, because everybody acknowledges that we are in a very messy situation and it has been woefully mismanaged. There is no real argument about that point from anywhere on the political spectrum. The problem is, it seems to me, to try to be fair to all the parties involved, and it doesn't help to presume the worst intentions on the part of anybody. The problem is there are genuine differences—I'm living in Washington during the summer and I'm seeing this in talking with friends and just picking up the tone of the city—there are genuine differences among people about what really will serve the best interests of the Iraqis. I think by Catholic principles, the real question is not, "What is good for America?" It's really, "What is good for Iraq?" I mean, we made the mess, not the Iraqis. We made the mess there. And after the failure of the rationale for weapons of mass destruction, really the argument for Iraq became humanitarian intervention: we were going to bring about regime change to remove an oppressive regime and bring about some sort of democratic set of institutions that had local legitimacy.

If you are going to do humanitarian intervention, that is a very different rationale than fighting a war of self-defense. If I am fighting for self-defense, the end or the goal of the war is simply to restore rights and my autonomy as a political community, that I have resisted those who threatened that. But if the purpose of war is humanitarian intervention, then the argument is we went in there to make their life better, not our life better. It seems to me, then, that what some of the rhetoric frankly that comes from the left on this—although I am, cards on the table, I am profoundly critical and was critical from the get-go about this and have written a fair amount on this whole question—but some of the criticism that comes from people who I think of as friends and political allies, I find disturbing because the argument is that we are losing too many troops, it is costing us too much money. The arguments are all self-referential for the United States. That we should leave because we are tired of it. I don't think that's an argument, a moral argument, to get out of Iraq.

I think the real argument is, "What best serves the Iraqi people's future now that we have so terribly ruined their present?" It seems to me there really are good and sincere arguments on both sides that we must leave because we are only exacerbating the tensions in the country, we're only encouraging further terrorism, we're only making Iraq a locus for international terrorism and the like. But there are also arguments that we need to stay because we have to create some sort of security before we leave, establish some sort of transitional government or regime that can hold things together, and I don't presume that people are saying that for terrible reasons, or for the worst of reasons. Are there bad arguments on the right for why we should stay? Yes. There are also bad arguments on the left for why we should get out. It seems that one of the things we have to acknowledge is that this is a case where very good and dedicated and selfless people really can disagree. But I think it was Kristin who earlier this morning was saying there are good and there are bad reasons; sometimes, there are bad reasons for doing good things.

I think we need to get out of Iraq because I do think the argument that we in fact are only making the situation worse by staying there is quite legitimate. I also think the argument that somehow we are omniscient—knowing that if we leave, this whole thing falls apart—presumes a knowledge of the region in Iraq now that we didn't have when we went in. I see no reason to think we are thinking any better about the situation now—that we can predict what will happen after we leave. But the point is there are good reasons to get out, but I think there are very profoundly wrong reasons, and I think reasons that are basically lodged in America's self-interest ignore the fact that we now claim we went in not for our interests but for the well-being of the Iraqis.

Richard Miller: Let me follow up on that and take some of the questions you asked Father Ken Himes from the end of your talk. One of those questions was, "When should our nation use or avoid the use of military force, for what purpose, under what authority, and at what human cost?" And let me add to that another question, "On Catholic principles, when should we do humanitarian intervention with a world full of nasty dictators oppressing their people?" The example given here is Rwanda. It is a little different but where you have genocide, that kind of thing. Sometimes the argument is, "Well, we can't be the policeman of the world."

Kenneth Himes: I think that is true. We can't be the policeman of the world. You know, this is one of the things I didn't have a chance to address because we got bogged down talking about Augustine and didn't get into talking about context. One of the things we all realize—everybody on this panel does and all of you do as well—is that the moral principles and the values of the Catholic social tradition always have to be applied contextually. You have to deal with the resources, the opportunities, the limitations, the restrictions that any historical context provides in the application of your principles and values.

In the abstract it is very easy to say, "Well, we should always act in such a way to defend and protect human rights and we must move into any situation of genocide." There are historical contexts that may make that a very bad idea for a particular nation to act on that at a given time and place. So, part of the problem here, it seems to me, is that I can talk in the abstract about those kinds of questions, but talking in the abstract about them doesn't really resolve a particular issue. To talk about any particular issue, you simply can't do that in five minutes or even thirty-five minutes, in terms of really looking at the context in which you are trying to apply principles and values. I suspect that is the frustration that all six of us felt at different points given the limitations of time and so on. You could teach a course on any one of the topics we were dealing with in thirty-five minutes. But let me say for the sake of putting it out there: My own view is that the Catholic tradition has seen a movement from a fairly broad range of rationales for why you could use military force to an increasingly narrower range of arguments for why one can use military force.

Indeed, it was fairly clear by the end of Pius XII's pontificate—for those of us who remember there was a guy named Pius XII—it was very clear that the only rationale the Vatican had given its support to was self-defense against aggression. And that tended to be sort of the defining characteristic of the Catholic just war tradition compared to other traditions, whose arguments were that this was not a case of *realpolitik*, that just war tradition is not simply rationalizations for countries to pursue their own self-interests narrowly. Indeed, it was trying to think through what are those limit cases where questions of competing goods or competing evils are there and people make hard decisions.

The judgment was that this is legitimate in cases of self-defense against aggression. What we have seen, it seems to me, interestingly and often from the left in that last fifteen years, have been arguments to expand the range of use of military force precisely for things like Bosnia or for Darfur today, in terms of humanitarian interventions. Not for self-defense against aggression, but to help people avert mass slaughter, ethnic cleansing, genocide, and the like. It is why I said it is a very tough issue because what we are really seeing now is another rationale for going to war precisely after a century in which we saw the range of reasons to go to war being narrowed in the Catholic tradition.

I think another issue that is looming on the horizon for us is the question of use of military force for the sake of nonproliferation of weapons of mass destruction. That is going to come back again. It wasn't just Iraq. You're going to hear those noises around Iran as it develops; you heard those noises around North Korea. That issue is going to return. What I see on the horizon simply is an ongoing argument on the part of many of us that the utility of military force is increasingly disproportionate to the harms it brings about. At the same time, people will be drawing up hard cases where at least you can make reasonably plausible arguments that some considered and discriminating use of force may in fact be less harmful than allowing various atrocities or various rogue states to engage in activities that threaten millions.

It is a very tough question, and I don't think you can settle it in the abstract. You have to look at the history of North Korea, or Iran, or Iraq, or these sorts of cases, or interventions in Darfur or Kosovo or Bosnia or the like, or Rwanda. It is not a matter that ultimately gets settled by the abstract principle but the argument of how to use those principles and values in very concrete situations.

Richard Miller: Dr. O'Brien.

David O'Brien: Just to add a little bit to that—the nonviolence movement is not dead, though the peace movement in the United States is kind of paralyzed at the moment. Around the world there is much research and much experimentation and discussion at fairly high levels about getting better at forms of nonviolent intervention in human rights and genocide-type situations, with early warning systems and forms of intervention before you need to have military intervention. And in that nonviolence area, the Holy Father, just about three weeks ago preaching on the love of enemies text, referred to it as the charter of Christian nonviolence and said that that charter was our call as Christians to nonviolence. I heard George Weigel and a group of friends getting very worried about the growth of interest in nonviolence in the Holy See this year.

The other source of some hope is the Catholic Peacebuilding Network. Kennon has talked about peace being a verb, being an action, and so on. The Catholic Peacebuilding Network is a developing network of people around the globe who are in grassroots situations—often of very great danger and jeopardy—who are trying to build peace in these situations. Catholic Relief Services and the University of Notre Dame have been encouraging and supporting that. They work with Mennonites, but if you Google the Catholic Peacebuilding Network, they had this summer in Colombia the fourth international meeting. That for me is one of the most encouraging things. I had the privilege of attending one of the early organizing meetings; these people are Catholics working with others in these dangerous situations and it is an inspiration to see, translating that peacemaking kind of idea into action.

Drew Christiansen: The Vatican is very interested in this. When we did the international Catholic-Mennonite dialogue, Pope John Paul II clearly had an interest because of the Mennonites' witness to nonviolence, so that section of the document really assumed a great deal of importance. The Mennonites, when it came to considering a second stage said, "Look, we're practical people. Theological dialogue is for Catholics. We don't know that many theologians. Let's do something practical." And the Vatican staff was divided as to how to respond because we don't usually do common projects. Well, they have decided that the Pontifical Council for Promoting Christian Unity and the Mennonite World Conference will do a joint contribution on alternatives to violence for the World Council of Churches' Decade Against Violence, at the conclusion of that in 2010. So it is a halfway house; it's something they're doing together that is more or less practical but it is not really on-the-ground practical; it's looking at alternatives to violence and doing it jointly.

Michael Himes: I'll just add one thing to something that my brother, Ken, said. Notice the growth of the idea that armed force might be used to go into a country in order to defend some group that is being oppressed or whose rights are being violated in the country—Darfur for example—presumes that human rights trump nation-states. It is another indication of that question that I raised a few moments ago: Are we seeing the gradual decline of the centrality of the nation-state as a way of understanding how human beings are organized around the globe?

It seems like a very strange question, and it affects globalization as well. We are so accustomed to think that, well of course you're a citizen of some country: You're a citizen of France or you're a citizen of South Africa. You're a citizen of Argentina or of the United States. But recognize that for a very long time in human history people weren't organized that way at all. Up until 140 years ago, there was no nation-state called Germany; there was no nation-state called Italy. There were Italians and Germans, and they lived in many cases very rich cultural lives, but they weren't members of nation-states. The assumption that that is how you organize communities, that's a particular way that emerged in Europe in the seventeenth century for organizing national life. Subsequently other parts of the globe have struggled, sometimes successfully and sometimes unsuccessfully, sometimes unrealistically, to form, to adapt themselves to it. Interestingly, in the place where it was born—Europe—it now seems to be passing away perhaps as a central way of organizing a community.

It affects the question of Iraq. I like to point out that my mother is turning eighty-eight next month. She was born in 1919. She is one year older than Iraq. There never was a country called Iraq until 1920. It was created largely by British and French influence as a way of dealing with the breakup of the Ottoman Empire. So when we talk about restoring the nation of Iraq, we are talking about a nation that as a nation-state is not as old as my mother! That notion of the nation-state and the inviolability of national borders, yeah, maybe. But I have a suspicion that over the course of the next 50 years we may see vast changes in that notion of the nation-state.

Richard Miller: This is for the whole panel and then we are coming to a close: "What specific political actions should Catholics focus on regarding the preferential option for the poor?"

David O'Brien: One thing I was going to say—my reaction time is about eight hours, so I will wake up tomorrow morning and have brilliant answers to all these questions—was that I sounded a little negative about some of the things going on at the bishops' conference, but there are really remarkable national agencies in the Catholic Church in the area of social ministry with tremendously talented and dedicated staffs—Catholic Relief Services, Catholic Charities USA, and the Office of Bishops' Conference. The Catholic Relief Services and the Bishops' Conference have launched a campaign against global poverty. They have a Web site, and they have remarkable materials that are available for local use—lots of ideas and projects that people can do locally that reflect some of the things that Jeffrey Sachs and others are suggesting. If you hear Jeffrey Sachs speak, he will just say buy mosquito nets, right? Buy mosquito nets, a very concrete kind of things to do.

As Kristin has mentioned, Catholic Charities has launched a new kind of national antipoverty campaign. CCHD has a Web site called Poverty US that is probably the best Web site in the country for up-to-date information about the poverty situation in the United States; there is also the Justice for Immigrants campaign. Again, these sites contain not just a lot of data and information but also very concrete materials for education and local use. A concrete thing to do regarding poverty would be to check the Catholic Campaign Against Global Poverty for suggestions for local education, local organization, such as having a coffee party at your house and getting everybody at that party to buy five mosquito nets or whatever Jeffrey Sachs and the others have lined up to do.

Drew Christiansen: One domestic and one national proposal. Domestically, I think an important contribution is being made by the living wage movement, and to support living wage legislation in your city, in your county, in your state. I think this is an important way to address the question of poverty. The minimum wage is just a token. On the international level, the Holy Father and heads of bishops' conferences pressing this government and all governments to make good on their commitment to the millennium development goals is really key. But remember, in the United States we have committed ourselves, as other countries have, and then not delivered. So the question is insisting that our country deliver on those goals and not just make oral promises. It is seeing it in the budget and seeing it allocated by the government. Those are really important.

Richard Miller: I want to thank our speakers. To indicate the brilliance of our speakers, they answered the questions before they were even asked. That's very impressive. I want to thank them all.

Appendix I

A Sampling of Written Questions Presented at the Symposium

Questions for Michael J. Himes, Ph.D.

1. If religion and politics should not be separated, how can liberal "Catholic" politicians be pro-abortion?
2. If religion and politics cannot (nor should not) be separated, why is there so much opposition by liberal Catholics to the Church making statements or taking a stand on political issues in this country, such as Amendment 2, on embryonic stem cell research, in Missouri?
3. Where do the bishops get the right to refuse Communion to people who are pro-choice? Jesus wants everyone to come to him.
4. Conscience means being informed from the other members of the community of values that contribute to our own and consequently to our decisions. Is it not also important to be informed by our "temporal" or historical community in the formation of our values and our conscience for decision-making?
5. If conscience is formed by community, what happens when the community is messed up?
6. Your thought on popular culture: constant media/entertainment, materialism, being self-absorbed, and constant public sexual themes. Does one build a wall against these influences or try to build a bridge to find and bring redemption into the secular city?
7. Your closing quotation from E. Burke on voting your conscience. Please comment on politicians who believe one way but vote the opposite because of the people they represent.
8. What does modern science—Galileo, Newton, etc.—do for classical understanding of life in common in the city-state? What impact does this have on religion and politics?
9. Why is it that some bishops insist that the measure of a well-formed conscience is whether or not my conscience agrees with theirs?

Questions for David J. O'Brien, Ph.D.

1. What suggestions do you have for guiding principles for Catholics in the future political process? What is the influence of Protestant evangelicals on "forming" evangelical Catholics as a strong activist element in American Catholicism?

2. If you had five minutes and were speaking to a group (with a "limited" vocabulary), what would be your simplified key message for a successfully striving for the goals set by the bishops' "Faithful Citizenship"?
3. Pronounce your definition of global pluralism and its theological implications.
4. Are there any U.S. bishops who will influence other bishops toward a broader, more liberal involvement in American life?

Questions for Kristin E. Heyer, Ph.D.

1. Do you have any suggestions about how grassroots people may come to understand and then act on the principles of the common good? For parish groups, local civic groups, youth groups, or maybe even religious communities?
2. How can the common good be expressed given a pluralistic society with many different ways of naming the good?
3. What is the difference between common good and public interest? What may be the implications of differences for community organizing?
4. This country was formed on each individual having certain inalienable rights. Are those rights in conflict with the common good?
5. In a simple and just form, what do you propose for the Mexican immigrants who want to live and work in the United States as citizens?
6. Elaborate on "eschatology," our common destiny.
7. Common good is local and global. Which has higher priority when they conflict?
8. Please speak to the views of younger Catholics (twenty- to forty-year-olds) regarding church affiliation and action for change, and political engagement or lack thereof.
9. Is the Catholic Church "compassionate conservative" or socialistic? What is the difference between an illegal immigrant and an undocumented immigrant?
10. Is the common good based on values that transcend a particular religious tradition? If so, on/by what authority? Help me think through globalization through a Catholic lens.

Questions for Rev. Kenneth Himes, O.F.M., Ph.D.

1. Is "just war" just an excuse for exercising political will?
2. How can anyone defend the war in Iraq as a "just war"? We have gone into a country we don't understand. What steps should we take to "understand" the Iraqis?

3. It seems that the U.S. bishops have been pretty silent about the war in Iraq. Any comment?
4. About a year before he became pope, Benedict said he believed World War II was a just war for Germany. Popes Pius XII and John Paul II believed World War II was a just war for the Allies. Is this relativism or just following informed conscience, or both?
5. On Catholic principle, when should we do humanitarian intervention with a world full of nasty dictators oppressing their people? Rwanda comes to mind.
6. Your statement on human rights, as broader than citizenship, seems to have implications regarding the issue of immigration. Could you elaborate?

Questions for Lisa Sowle Cahill, Ph.D.

1. How do you influence "one-issue abortion Catholics" to see the big picture? How do all pro-life issues overlap?
2. Why did the change from emphasis on pro-abortion to pro-choice occur?
3. Is there a difference in principles and process between personal ethics and social ethics?

Questions for Rev. Drew Christiansen, S.J., Ph.D.

1. You've articulated general principles of sustainable development but have stopped short of any suggestions of specific actions. Give us examples of actions that confirm these principles.
2. In what way would presentations differ if this took place at Liberty University or Oral Roberts University?

Questions for All Speakers

1. How would you outline a voting strategy for 2008 for Catholics in light of the bishops' pastoral letter? Especially on immigration?
2. Religious fundamentalists seem to see a simple world—black and white, good and evil, Scripture and "popery." This seems an effective approach for political mobilization. How can people considering the complex interrelationships of the bishops' fifty-plus issues ever master the kind of unanimity of mind necessary to build powerful majorities?
3. "American" Catholics, "American" politics, "American" culture, "American" people." I assume "American" means those of us in the United States. Have you any idea how we have come to be Americans

and other Americans are Mexican Americans, Canadian Americans, Nicaraguans, Hondurans, and so forth? It does not make sense to me.

4. How do we, the faithful, urge or influence the bishops to support their own document?
5. Why are lay ministers and women considered second-class citizens in the Church? Is the hierarchy threatened?
6. The role of politics in preaching at Mass: Please share your thoughts on time at Mass being used to tell people how to vote on a certain issue. I attend Mass and bring my children to deepen our spirituality and learn more about God, not to be told what vote to cast as if I can't make my own decisions.
7. Could you comment on Garry Wills' book, *What Jesus Meant?* The basic gist of it seems to be that Jesus was not political.
8. The concept of intrinsic moral evil was used by Archbishop Burke of St. Louis and others to support their argument for the absolute priority of five issues. Please respond to that; is the concept misused by that use of it?
9. As Catholics, how do we remind our church and each other to focus on all five moral priorities of the bishops' letter on voting, rather than continue to focus only on a select few issues?
10. How do we respond (dialogue) with bishops who speak publicly about excommunication for voting for certain candidates? How do we handle the public embarrassment?
11. With the statistics of Dr. Miller's opening challenge, might we worry (more) about the percentage of Catholics joining the literal biblical believers? Is grassroots (at the family table) the best teaching time? Are our priests and pastors encouraged at priests' events to speak to this? Should I get my sewing machine ready to make burqas? (This is a woman asking this!)
12. Common good should include equal rights for women in the Catholic Church, specifically, if a woman is called to the priesthood, she should not be denied because of gender!
13. Who at this point in the political calendar do you see most representing a Catholic position on most of the important moral issues?
14. How can one navigate through political homelessness and maintain integrity and dignity?
15. How to deal with and overcome radical Islamic jihadists who have a culture of death and will never accept ideas of common good and relational harmony? Why do peaceful Muslims allow radical Muslims to define how the world views their religion and religious goals?

16. As a family life ministry professional, I find it difficult to recruit "pro-life" people to volunteer for Birthright and being there for the moms. Their interest seems more in placards and politicians.
17. Please comment on EWTN influence in our Church.
18. Has the war in Iraq destroyed Christianity freedom in Iraq? How many abortions did the falling of bombs cause?
19. Why is it that when a person moves to the rigid side of our Church, he or she is blessed? If you move to the free or Spirit-led side of our Church, you are looked upon with suspicion.
20. Why don't we teach these values and concepts in our Catholic high schools?
21. Conscience certainly becomes complex when you introduce the community and common good. Add to this an ordinary who seeks to impose his version of the issue, and you have more than most Catholics in the pew can handle. Any ideas as to which percentage of each you would advise?
22. Why aren't these values preached in our Catholic churches on Sundays?
23. How would you deal with the claim that abortion is per se evil and therefore the primary determining issue in choosing a candidate to vote for?
24. Can you build an absolute teaching on a probable theological principle? Concretely, if John Paul II is correct in calling ensoulment at conception a probable theological position, can other "timing" of ensoulment also be reasonably justifiable?
25. In terms of our nation's "common good," undocumented immigrants are illegal immigrants. We are carrying their burden by paying for their education, health care, and child care needs. How do we tackle this issue for the common good?
26. What is the Church's position on illegal immigration?
27. How do we deal with correcting the dominance of economic influences—you saw this in the stem cell debate. How does the dominance of capitalism relate to Catholicism and the American experience?
28. What specific political actions should Catholics focus on regarding the preferential option for the poor?
29. I noted with gratitude that you studiously spoke in inclusive terms about God and humans in the first half of your talk. Then you slipped into "he" more than once. Is it difficult to avoid nonsexist language in Church circles?

Appendix II

Religion and Politics Web Sites

The best sources of information on religion and politics can be accessed through the Web site of the Pew Forum on Religion and Public Life (www.pewforum.org). Excellent voting data are available from the Zogby polling firm (www.zogby.com) and from John Green at the Ray C. Bliss Institute of Applied Politics at the University of Akron (www.uakron.edu/bliss/). William D'Antonio at the Life Cycle Institute contests some of the current data on Catholic attitudes. He may be contacted at wdantonio@cua.edu.

Election Year 2004 produced www.catholicsforkerry.org and www.kerrywrongforcatholics.org. There were many initiatives, one of the best of which was www.responsiblecitizenship.org. For a humorous take try www.cafeteriacatholics.com.

Check out Republicans (www.rnc.org and www.gop.com), where you will find a link for the "Catholic Team." The election year links are gone for now, but the work goes on. For impressive organizing see www.priestsforlife.org, and a growing e-mail action network, Fidelis (www.fidelis.org). The irrepressible Dale Hudson is back, at www.morleyicc.org.

Conservative Catholic strategies can be followed in the national column of George Weigel and in the column of editor Richard Neuhaus in *First Things*. There is nothing comparable on the Catholic center or left. The annual, supposedly nonpolitical, Catholic prayer breakfast, is organized by GOP operatives and for several years featured a talk by President Bush, whose achievements are highlighted on the Web site. This year Anthony Cardinal Bevilacqua served as advisor and Washington Archbishop Donald Wuerl as host (www.catholicprayerbreakfast.org).

With the Democrats (www.democrats.org or www.dnc.org), Catholic groups and strategies are hard to find although the Party has hired John Kelly as a Catholic outreach person (kellyj@dnc.org). An independent group with an impressive website is Catholic Democrats (www.catholicdemocrats.org). John Podesta's Center for American Progress www.americanprogress.org, a Democratic Party think tank, respects Catholic concerns.

On consistent ethic of life, check www.consistent-ethic.org and www.democratsforlife.org, where you will find interesting new bipartisan strategies for reducing abortions.

For bishops, see www.usccb.org, especially the Department of Social Development and World Peace, where you will find references to statements by the bishops on many issues and their campaigns on immigration and global poverty. You can also check department listings for Pro-Life Activities and "Faithful Citizenship." Their poverty program, the Catholic Campaign for Human Development (www.usccb.org/cchd) maintains one of the nation's best sources of information on poverty. Just add "povertyusa" to the last Web listing. Catholic Charities-USA (www.catholicchartiesusa.org), the professional organization of diocesan Catholic Charities personnel, has launched a campaign against domestic poverty, while Catholic Relief Services (www.crs.org), the nation's largest private sector overseas relief and development agency, has launched with the Bishops Conference a Catholic Campaign to End Global Poverty (www.usccb.org/sdwp/globalpoverty). A good state Web site is Michigan's (www.micatholicconf.org/public-policy).

In 2004, Catholic Answers (www.catholicanswers.org) produced a voter guide alternative to the bishops' "Faithful Citizenship," urging conscience formation on the basis of a set of "nonnegotiable" issues: abortion, embryonic stem cells, euthanasia and assisted suicide, and gay marriage. For continued leadership from this side, see www.caaction.org. A similar effort, favored by the Massachusetts bishops, is former Boston Mayor and U.S. Ambassador to the Vatican Ray Flynn's Catholic Citizenship (www.catholicvote.org). This is a valuable Web site with news and links with emphasis on abortion, gay marriage and other issues, including capital punishment. This group spearheads the fight against gay marriage here in Massachusetts.

Backing the Bernardin-era consistent life ethic and "Faithful Citizenship" is Catholics in Alliance for the Common Good (www.catholicsinalliance.org) and its more active partner, Catholics United for the Common Good (www.catholics-united.org). The group also sponsors a source for political news (www.catholicmediareport.org).

Jim Wallis is of course the progressive voice within the Evangelical community and spearheads interfaith efforts, including "The Covenant for a New America." His work can be found through Sojourners (www.sojo.org).

Conservative Christian voices can be found at Focus on the Family (www.family.org and www.focusaction.org), the Christian Coalition of America (www.christiancoalition.com), the Moral Majority Coalition (www.moralmajority.com), and the energetic Pat Robertson (www.patrobertson.org).

Appendix III

Speakers' Biographies

Lisa Sowle Cahill, Ph.D.

Lisa Sowle Cahill grew up primarily in northern Virginia. She completed her undergraduate studies at the University of Santa Clara and her doctorate at the University of Chicago. She is the prestigious J. Donald Monan Professor in the Theology Department at Boston College, where she has taught since 1976. She has also been a visiting professor at Georgetown and Yale Universities. She and her husband Larry are the parents of five children. Dr. Cahill is past president of the Catholic Theological Society of America and has served as a consultant to the National Conference of Catholic Bishops Marriage and Family Life Committee. Recently she was elected to the American Academy of Arts and Sciences. Her books and research interests often end in the word "ethics" and include history of Christian ethics; New Testament and ethics; Catholic social ethics; sex and gender ethics; bioethics; and ethics of war and peace. In the past five years she has written or edited five books, as well as literally dozens of articles and not all of them in English. In 2005 the Catholic Press Association gave their First Place Award for Theology to her publication: *Theological Bioethics: Participation, Justice, and Change.*

Reverend Drew Christiansen, S.J., Ph.D.

Father Drew Christiansen, S.J., currently serves as editor-in-chief of *America* magazine. Over the years, he has headed the USCCB Office of International Justice and Peace and served as their counselor for international affairs. He was also the lead staff person drafting the bishops' 1993 peace pastoral, "The Harvest of Justice Is Sown in Peace." Father Christiansen has served in several appointed, key positions for ecumenical endeavors for the Holy See. His doctorate in religious social ethics is from Yale, and he has twice been a fellow at the Woodstock Theological Center in Washington, D.C. His book on the theological ethics of family caregiving to the elderly it titled *When All My Strength Is Spent.* He also is co-editor of the USCCB "And God Saw It Was Good: Catholic Theology and the Environment" (1996) and was the U.S. bishops' principal advisor for their 1991 pastoral statement on the environment.

Kristin W. Heyer, Ph.D.

Kristin Heyer spent many of her formative years in Kansas City attending Visitation Parish School and Pembroke Hill before returning to the East Coast to Brown University. She worked two years at the Department of Justice in Washington and then earned her doctorate in theological ethics at Boston College. Currently she is on the theology faculty at Loyola Marymount University in Los Angeles. Her book, *Prophetic & Public: The Social Witness of U.S. Catholicism,* recently received the Catholic Theological Society's award for best book of 2006. Dr. Heyer has published more than ten articles and reviews and presented at a dozen professional conferences, a law school seminar, and other groups on various dimensions of social ethics. She has received several grants for researching pertinent issues in ethics such as AIDS and immigration. Recently Roger Cardinal Mahoney appointed her to the Theological Committee for the Archdiocese of Los Angeles.

Reverend Kenneth R. Himes, O.F.M., Ph.D.

Father Kenneth Himes is Professor and Chair of the Theology Department at Boston College. He was previously on the faculty at Washington Theological Union. A member of the Order of Friars Minor (Franciscans), he spent twenty-four years in Washington, D.C., many of those years teaching at Washington Theological Union, in addition to holding a number of leadership positions within his religious community. Father Himes has been a consultant to the U.S. Bishops' Conference where for several years he served as theological consultant for their Office of Social Development and World Peace. His research interests are in the history of Catholic social teaching, the role of the U.S. Catholic community in American social reform, the ethics of warfare, and the relationship of religion and politics in the nation's public life. His books include *Responses to 101 Questions on Catholic Social Teaching* and *Modern Catholic Social Teaching: Commentaries and Interpretations.*

Reverend Michael J. Himes, Ph.D.

Father Himes is Professor of Theology at Boston College. His books include *Fullness of Faith: The Public Significance of Theology,* which he coauthored with his brother, Father Kenneth Himes, O.F.M., and which was awarded the Catholic Press Association Book Award; *Doing Truth in Love: Conversations About God, Relationships, and Service;* and *Ongoing Incarnation: Johann Adam Mohler and the Beginnings of Modern Ecclesiology,* which received the Catholic Press Association Book Award in 1998. He has also written several popular video series: *The Mystery of Faith: An Introduction to Catholicism, Questions of the Soul, The Vision of the Gospels,* and *The Vision of Vatican II for Today.*

Richard W. Miller, Ph.D.

Richard Miller is an Assistant Professor of Systematic Theology at Creighton University. He began his academic career at the University of Notre Dame with a B.A. in theology and philosophy and then received an M.A. and Ph.D. in systematic theology from Boston College. He is one of the founders of this lecture series and has been a contributor to and editor of the published versions of this series: *Prayer in the Catholic Tradition* (2007), *Spirituality for the 21st Century: Experiencing God in the Catholic Tradition* (2006), and *Lay Ministry in the Catholic Church: Visioning Church Ministry through the Wisdom of the Past* (2005). He also contributed *to The Catholic Church in the 21st Century: Finding Hope for its Future in the Wisdom of Its Past* (2004), which was edited by Michael J. Himes.

David O'Brien, Ph.D.

David O'Brien is Loyola Professor of Roman Catholic Studies at College of the Holy Cross. He was the founding director of the Center for Religion, Ethics and Culture at Holy Cross. He has been a faculty member there since 1969. Dr. O'Brien holds six honorary degrees and received the Theodore M. Hesburgh Award for distinguished service to Catholic higher education from the Association of Catholic Colleges and Universities. He is a historian specializing in the history of Catholicism in the United States, particularly Catholic social and political thought and religion and politics. He has been quoted in numerous publications, including *The New York Times, The Washington Post,* and Associated Press articles. He has also written numerous op-ed pieces for *The Boston Globe* and *Worcester Telegram & Gazette,* among others. The author of several books, Dr. O'Brien frequently provides expert commentary for the media. His books include *Catholic Social Thought: The Documentary Heritage; American Catholics and Social Reform: The New Deal Years; The Renewal of American Catholicism;* and *Public Catholicism.*